Maillot Jaune

Original title: *Le Maillot Jaune*
© 1999 Copyright Studio, Paris, France
© 2001 VeloPress, Boulder, Colorado, USA, for the American edition
Translation: Roland Glasser and John Wilcockson

Printed in Spain

Distributed in the United States and Canada by Publishers Group West

International Standard Book Number: 1-884737-98-6

Library of Congress Cataloging-in-Publication Data

Ollivier, Jean Paul, 1944-
[Maillot jaune. English]
Maillot jaune : the Tour de France yellow jersey / Jean-Paul Ollivier.
p. cm.
Includes index.
ISBN 1-884737-98-6
1. Tour de France (Bicycle race)—History.   I. Title.

GV1049.2.T68 O44 2001
796.6'2'0944—dc21   00-068588

VeloPress
1830 North 55th Street
Boulder, Colorado 80301-2700 USA
303/440-0601; Fax 303/444-6788; E-mail velopress@7dogs.com

To purchase additional copies of this book or other VeloPress books, call 800/234-8356 or visit us on the Web at velopress.com.

Maillot Jaune

The Tour de France Yellow Jersey

Jean-Paul Ollivier

VELO
press®

Boulder, Colorado   USA

CONTENTS

FOREWORD

The 1957 Tour de France had just reached Colmar, the finish of the seventh stage. Eight cyclists had broken away from the peloton and crossed the line, boosted by a sudden desire for independence, here in the birthplace of Bartholdi, sculptor of the Statue of Liberty. Nothing strange about that. All eyes were fixed on a young Italian kid from Paris with a rather noble Italian name: Nicolas Barone. Taking advantage of the insolent strength of the French national team, Barone had just pinched the prestigious yellow jersey off Jacques Anquetil, then a young professional of 23, by 38 seconds. Nicolas was crying like a baby: "Maillot jaune!" A lifetime's dream. One after another, his teammates Jean Bobet, Stanislas Bober, Guy Million, André Le Dissez rushed up to warmly embrace him, but he was in another world and didn't even hear radio reporter Georges Briquet shouting at the top of his voice, while holding back from asking Nicolas what he was feeling....

"Dear listeners, Nicolas Barone is crying with emotion...." Draped in the yellow jersey, he was secretly dreaming of someone else. "What's your fiancé's name?" ventured the journalist. "Paulette," Barone quietly replied, swallowing his tears, "Paulette Deshays." The questions stopped there and he went back to his hotel, floating on the sweet fragrance of the moment. Jean Mazier, his team director, who everyone called "Tonton Jean," knew his heavy secret. Paulette was shunned by the Barone family. They found every fault in her: not having Italian roots, being common, leading a sordid life even....

That evening, gathered around the dinner table, Tonton Jean cleared his throat and struck his glass with a fork. You could have sworn that he had slipped a bit of Napoleon into his speech: "Kids, I'm pleased with you. I am proud of Nicolas. This yellow jersey will help him win the battles of his life and his love!" It was nicely said and very true, for there have been so many miracles associated with the maillot jaune.

Some of this mysterious alchemy even rubbed off on a few animals, as happened at Aurillac, one evening in 1959. The peloton that had come from Albi after countless battles through the Auvergne hills, dubbed the Flemish rider Jos Hoevenaers "the bulldog" after he came forward to bow gravely before the yellow jersey waiting for him on the podium. Hoevenaers had good reason to celebrate, but he was also aware of the risks and torment to come. Not only did the courageous Jos know that others, more able and more Machiavellian, would grab the emblem from him the next day, but destiny obliged him to spend the night in the *Hotel Terminus*....

So Jos retired quietly to his room, leaving the door ajar and invitingly open to any visitors. In the suffocating night of the Cantal's principal city, a visitor quietly slipped in. The darkness closed heavily around the peacefully sleeping new Tour leader. It was only in the morning that the Belgian noticed an unusual snoring sound. On the empty bed next to his, an old cocker spaniel had curled up in the yellow jersey to snooze. One would have thought that the woolen jersey had been woven especially for him, since the dog slept on undisturbed.

Jos woke him up and was suddenly dumb struck. The blind cocker spaniel raised his expressionless, chalky eyes as if begging for a few more minutes of rest. Jos let him lie there for as long as possible. When the Belgian finally left, it was as if the yellow jersey had once more worked its magic, since the cocker spaniel headed straight for the light.

> "This morning, I gave a superb yellow jersey to courageous Christophe. You already know that our director has decided that the man who leads the general classification will wear a jersey in the colors of *L'Auto*. The fight for possession of the jersey will be fierce."
>
> —Henri Desgrange, L'Auto, *1919*

Did Henry Desgrange, father of the Tour de France and head of *L'Auto* newspaper realize, when he created this eye-catching garment in 1919, that he was also creating a potent symbol of hope, as if a flag had suddenly risen from the war's still-fresh trenches? But this emblem was that of a rediscovered peace, which all believed would last forever.

Once more the great adventure set off across the soil of a weary France, now reduced to a network of potholed and neglected old roads. There was a shortage of tires, and cars were few, but the whole population cheered on the tourmen, with Henri Pélissier as their standard-bearer. But the time had come for innovation. Desgrange received complaints that his creation whizzed by too fast. One hardly had time to make out the leader and the Tour had already passed, leaving pleasure but also disappointment in its wake. "We want to see the leader!" This kind of remark was not lost on the father of the Tour.

In 1919, the problem became more vexing when, during the fourth stage from Brest to Les Sables d'Olonne, Henri Pélissier, the Tour leader, withdrew. While it had been childishly easy to recognize Pélissier's strong face, his successor, Eugène Christophe, had always remained in the background. So Desgrange turned the problem over in his head and inspiration hit him in two waves.

First, he announced in the July 10 issue of the *L'Auto*, just when the Luchon to Perpignan stage was starting, the creation of a distinctive emblem to be worn by the race leader. Second, he announced its color: it would be yellow, just like his newpaper. The order was placed, and knitting started on the first yellow jerseys. In Grenoble, on July 18, six woolen jerseys in a beautiful canary yellow lay spread out across Desgrange's desk, before he hurried off to award one of them to Christophe, who was still holding on firmly to the race leadership. That day was a rest day for the Tour in the city dear to the french author Stendahl.

Thus commenced an epic time, which mixed flesh and blood, the beautiful dawn and the sad evening, grandeur and servitude; but "glory never shines without virtue," said Antonin Magne. Magne, the ex-champion who became the directeur sportif of the man who would battle for the yellow jersey without ever grasping it: Raymond Poulidor. The Tour de France now provided the perfect setting for peacetime heroes. A wonderful idea. Isn't it said that genius is to be found in the simplest of endeavors, particularly if they attain the greatest meaning with the most popular intentions?

A true cult object, the yellow jersey caused the cycling cavalry to come at a gallop, everyone wanting to grab it, hug it, kiss it.... Cursed be the one who would never know this joy, like in the 1949 Tour when the Belgian Norbert Callens, victim of his absentminded *soigneur* who sent off the team's support truck with the yellow jersey in it, never had the honor of actually wearing it. The yellow jersey was left…well…jersey-less! Fortunately, the Belgian journalist Albert Van Laethem was just next to him, wearing a yellow sweater. Albert quickly pulled it off and handed it over, but there was no consoling Norbert, who would regret the event for the rest of his life.

No doubt, he'd be in complete agreement with the words of Jacques Goddet: "Always love and respect this emblem which personifies the strength of modern man just as it symbolizes the effort of the champion in our Tour."

> "The idea of the yellow jersey and the awarding of the prizes, stands out in my mind. I have even dreamed of Henri Desgrange himself, dressed as an inspector of the academy, handing over this precious trophy. And to little Darrigade who succeeded as well, without doubt."
> —*Michel Clare*, l'Equipe, 1958

The Pioneer

Eugène Christophe,
the first buttercup

Eugène Christophe was the first to wear the yellow jersey, but bad luck prevented him from ever winning the Tour.

Neither wind nor rain could stop Christophe. His popularity was enormous. The crowds nicknamed him "Cri-Cri."

"**N**o one has done as much for our sport as you have, Cri-Cri. With you we have lost a missionary for the sport of cycling. The generations that knew you will miss the exemplary man that you were."

These words were spoken by Antonin Magne during the funeral of Eugène Christophe, on February 6, 1970.

Just eighteen years old in 1903 when Henri Desgrange created the Tour de France, he made his debut two years later, alongside the stars of the time: Trousselier, Petit-Breton, Lapize, Thys, Georget, Pottier, Garigou, Faber, and others. But it was not until the famous generation of cyclists who emerged following the 1914-1918 war, that "the Old Gaul"—as he was called in reference to his moustache—became better known.

In 1919, Christophe became *l'éclaireur,* the one who was the first to open up the way to the yellow jersey. Leader of the race since the fourth stage, after the inglorious withdrawal of Henri Pélissie—who demanded, in vain, that at mealtimes the organizers of the Tour should serve something better than "sour wine costing 19½ cents"—Christophe looked likely to win the Tour; he got through the Pyrenees and the Alps without a hitch, and in Grenoble, which was a rest day, received the henceforth distinctive symbol of the leader in the general classification: the yellow jersey.

His 2 a.m. arrival at the start line of the eleventh stage from Grenoble to Geneva (200 miles) was a scene that he would never forget: "What have I got?" he would later recount, "Ah, the yellow jersey! What a lovely color, this canary yellow! What's Mrs. Cri-Cri doing at the moment?" And it went on like that for the rest of the day.

On the banks of Lake Geneva, Christophe posed in yellow for the first time. The magazine *La Vie au grand air (Life in the Great Outdoors)* decided to put him on the cover. This was the first printed image—in color—of the yellow jersey.

The wearer of the canary-colored jersey had final victory in sight. His strength was such that he appeared unbeatable. And yet…

On July 25, in the black of night, the starter gave the signal for the penultimate stage, Metz to Dunkirk. They worried about technical problems, since almost 100 miles of the stage was lined with cobblestones. But Christophe seemed so strong that even his most fearsome rival, the Belgian Firmin Lambot, could not imagine that any kind of upset was possible.

Suddenly, just as the race director's car was crossing the Valenciennes suburbs, Henri Manchon, Henri Desgrange's assistant, pointed out to the Tour boss a group of cyclists that was lagging behind.

The long open touring car came to a halt, and they saw a short mustachioed man, wearing a faded yellow jersey, pushing a bicycle with a broken fork.

Eugène Christophe just could not accept his awful destiny.

"Is there a forge around here?" he asked.

"Over here, monsieur," said a kid. There was a little bicycle workshop nearby.

"I'd like to know the size of your fork tubes," the cyclist asked the workshop owner.

And so the Old Gaul immediately set to work in the darkened room. For one hour and ten minutes he heated the metal until it was white-hot, hammered it, straightened it and filed it down. According to the rules, no one was allowed to help him. The various assistants watched without a word, stepping aside at the right moment so as not to impede his work, gripped by the emotion and grandeur of this spectacle of an athlete refusing to bow before a stroke of bad luck.

When he set off again, he had lost the yellow jersey.

The next day, as the Belgian Firmin Lambot carried off the Tour, the race definitively turned its back on Eugène Christophe, credited with the record for the most number of punctures.

Faced with such a succession of misadventures, *L'Auto* launched a fund with the aim of putting right "a misfortune that is unequalled in the history of the Tour." This was a guaranteed success, requiring the publication of twenty lists of donors. From Dr. Henri de Rothschild who gave 500 francs, to the twin brothers of Châtelguyon who gave 3 francs, many French people from all walks of life dug their hands into their pockets to show their sympathy for the first yellow jersey in history. He would receive a total of 13,310 francs, a much larger sum than that awarded to the winner.

So the adventures of a "master blacksmith" went down in history, as the first ever yellow jersey of the Tour de France.

Christophe admiring the yellow jersey, which assured him his place in history as its first holder.

Christophe in the company of two of his prestigious successors in the conquest of the golden fleece: Louison Bobet and Jacques Anquetil.

The Cannibal

"There was Merckx...and then everyone else." How many times have we heard this statement, expressed with admiration but sometimes with irritation or despondency by followers of the sport or cyclists themselves.

Previous page: ...and so began the regal breakaway (Luchon to Mourenx, Tour de France 1969).

Opposite: He excelled in all disciplines, fearing neither heat nor cold, rivaling the climbers, whom he even overpowered sometimes, and shrugging off any sprinter.

Tour 1969. Merckx let no one else take over the command. Gimondi suffered. A mutual esteem would always unite the two men.

Eddy Merckx, total domination

Magnificent, vulnerable and secret, Eddy Merckx's peaceful exterior hid a worried and tormented soul.

n 1969, Eddy Merckx's desire to make the Tour de France his prime goal of the season resulted in him easing up on his program at the start of the year. His reputation had already reached such a level that he was no longer able to take part in a major international race without having to fight, hoisting himself to the highest level. He had already won the Tour of Italy, the World Championship, Milan-San Remo…

He was still a member of the Italian Faema team, which had practically become a Belgian group, considering who rode on it. The cunning Guillaume Driessens became its directeur sportif and undertook a program of psychological training of the utmost importance, hiding from no one his intention to build a monolithic block: all for Merckx.

A new era in cycling was establishing itself. On the Col d'Eze, during the final stage time trial of Paris to Nice, the young Belgian literally took off, managing to catch and then pass Jacques Anquetil.

"That evening," he remembers, "I preferred not to look at Jacques, who was suffering. If I hadn't been in danger of losing the stage, then I would have avoided catching him, but Poulidor was still a threat…"

This was no time to be sentimental, particularly since during the Tour of Italy the Brussels wonder boy was accused of using and then positively tested for drugs. He was disqualified and left claiming his innocence. He would eventually be cleared, after a certain number of irregularities were found in the testing procedures.

Wounded but bent on revenge, he arrived at Roubaix for the start of the Tour de France. For the 6½-mile prologue time trial, the Faema team got the number one place by a drawing of lots. Driessens decided that its first man to start would be Eddy, a controversial decision since the first one to leave has no idea of the pace of his rivals. But wasn't Merckx surely the strongest? The sun was shining. The faster he got back, the sooner he could rest up in the afternoon.

From his very first Tour de France, Merckx claimed success for Belgium, thirty years after Sylvère Maës. It was the start of a long reign.

So Merckx headed off. In the last 3 miles he had to fight through a violent wind that most of his rivals missed as the day wore on. The German Rudi Altig beat him by 6 seconds.

But this disappointment was soon wiped clean since, on the second day of the race, upon arrival at his hometown of Woluwé-Saint-Pierre, he took the first yellow jersey of his career, at the end of a 9½-mile half-stage team time trial.

So this was the famous yellow jersey, still made of wool. However, the initials H.D. of the "Father of the Tour" had moved from the left breast to appear on each sleeve. A sponsor's name (Virlux) appeared on the famous shirt, while the manufacturer's logo was still kept (Le Coq Sportif).

Merckx knew that it is never a good idea to lead a stage race from the beginning, since one then has to shoulder all of the responsibility. He thus agreed to cede his golden jersey to his teammate Julien Stevens, who inherited it at Maastricht. He would keep it for three days.

Merckx bided his time before striking his first deadly blow. For his arena he chose the Ballon d'Alsace, in the Vosges mountains.

He made a lightning attack. Four men settled into his wake: Roger De Vlaeminck, Altig, Rini Wagtmans and Joaquin Galera. But they didn't hang on for long and Merckx triumphed alone. He had shown his mettle, but the Tour was far from over. Roger Pingeon, fighting a supremacy that he had always said was more of an illusion than a reality, kept up with the leader all the way over the Forclaz Pass and beat him in the sprint at Chamonix.

Pingeon would be his most dangerous rival, but the yellow jersey wouldn't let go of his precious woolen tunic, adding a new exploit on the stage that crossed the four passes in the Pyrenees from Luchon to Mourenx.

The ascent of the Col du Tourmalet started calmly enough, with the best riders grouped together. It was only when they were 200 meters from the summit that Merckx decided to accelerate so as to pass under the summit banner a few seconds ahead of his teammate Martin Van den Bossche and Pingeon, Zimmermann, Poulidor, Gutty, Bayssière, Theillière and Gandarias. The others, including Gimondi who was having some trouble, followed farther behind.

On the descent, the yellow jersey continued to accelerate.

The finish was still far off and so, for a moment, he wondered whether to keep up the pace, then gathered his strength and settled into a comfortable rhythm that didn't strain his ability. Even at this pace, he couldn't see anyone coming. Then, suddenly, he tightened his toe straps, brought

himself back up to speed and gave it his all. At the foot of the Aubisque, his lead had lengthened to over a minute. At the summit, it had reached 8 minutes, and there were still 45 relatively easy miles left to go. He kept this lead over his pursuers right up to the finish. Race director Jacques Goddet, never one for superlatives, called it: "Merckxissimo." As for writer Antoine Blondin, he referred to "the planet Merckx."

Thirty years after Sylvère Maës, Merckx brought Tour success back to Belgium.

In 1970, he didn't waste time and grabbed the yellow jersey in the prologue. It was simply a question of prestige. He was the violent pedaler par excellence, yet this violence was carefully channeled, balanced and transformed into efficient energy. He had already taken on the mantle of a Tour conqueror.

On the third day of the race, he passed the leader's jersey to his teammate, the Italian Italo Zilioli, so as to be free of such a heavy burden until they reached the mountain stages.

Hired from across the Alps by the Belgian after the 1969 Tour of Italy, Zilioli had, until then, been the repository of all Italian cycling dreams: "A new Coppi is born," the papers cried in 1963. Three times he finished second in the Giro.

In the flat stages, Merckx's Faemino team proved itself to be above reproach, although the yellow jersey didn't exempt Zilioli from doing his share of the team's work. The Italian would eventually lose his trophy at Valenciennes, at the end of the sixth stage, where Merckx—the "boss"—asserted his authority. Zilioli ran into one misfortune after another, capping them all with a puncture. No one waited for him, but he was careful not to show too much bitterness. He had lived a beautiful dream and, from now on, the stage was set for the Technicolor spectacular of the Faemino leader.

No one else would challenge him for the golden vest. Every day he fired some new salvos. Poulidor seemed disillusioned: "Every day he sets up the guillotine," he sighed, "and then places our head on the block."

Everyone attempted to find a chink in the armor, but to no avail. He won the time trials, flat stages and on Mont Ventoux, as well as the time trial on the last day, finishing the Tour as he had started it, in total domination, and carrying off the Tour of Italy-Tour de France double into the bargain.

In 1971, Merckx changed teams: Faema withdrew from competition and the Belgian champion signed with Molteni. Taking the yellow jersey right from the Mulhouse prologue—it was becoming a habit—he ceded it the following day to his teammate Rini Wagtmans, who well deserved

Roger Pingeon was one of Eddy Merckx's toughest adversaries. But in 1969, in full ascent, the young Belgian had no doubts whatsoever.

Tour de France 1969, the Luchon to Mourenx stage. After a breakaway of 87 miles, Merckx had KO'd the peloton. Jacques Goddet called it "Merckxissimo."

Tour 1970. Eddy's "red guard": with Guillaume Driessens, directeur sportif, Antheunis, Bruyère, Huysmans, Mintjens, Spruyt, Swerts, Van den Berghe, Van Schil and Zilioli.

this homage, having finished fifth in the previous Tour. The Dutchman was one hell of a downhill specialist and as soon as the road started to dip, his tuft of white hair could be seen forging ahead of the peloton. He was, without a doubt, one of the best "plungers" of all time.

He would only have a third of a stage to savor the feeling, since Merckx ensured that his "property" was very quickly returned, but he was one of Eddy's very close inner circle and would have the opportunity to taste more glory a little later, thanks to a great stage win on the velodrome at Nancy track.

Adversity did not get in the way of the esteem that Guimard the green jersey, Merckx the yellow jersey and Raymond Poulidor had for each other.

A serious battle raged for the first few days. This was when the Peugeot cyclist Christian Raymond baptized Merckx "the Cannibal"—a nickname apparently originating from his daughter, who affirmed that the Belgian won everything like a "real cannibal."

But it seemed that the man from Brussels was not showing his best face that year. The domination that Luis Ocaña had shown at the summit of the Puy-de-Dôme clearly asserted itself during the stage from Grenoble to Orcières-Merlette. The yellow jersey reign of the Spaniard from Mont-de-Marsan was beginning. He would, unfortunately, miss final victory, crashing out in a thunderstorm on the Col de Menté. Merckx thus took his third Tour de France without too much of a fight.

In 1972, the Merckx-Ocaña duel was eagerly awaited. It would not take place. Once again, Merckx took his first yellow jersey in the prologue, through the streets of Angers, beating the Spaniard by 15 seconds. Even though he lost the jersey the next day, at Saint-Brieuc, he dominated the Spaniard completely who, it must be said, was suffering from some serious breathing problems.

In the Pau-Luchon stage, Merckx's victory was applauded by everyone. He commenced his attack just before the Peyresourde summit, caught up with Lucien Van Impe on the descent and took the yellow jersey. He never gave it up, winning his fourth Tour and repeating the Tour of Italy-Tour de France double. He led his *Grande Boucle* with exemplary flair, always keeping the race in hand, controlling it and guiding it as he wished. His perceptiveness was as razor sharp as his style.

The appearance of the yellow jersey itself had changed. Henceforth the initials H.D. would appear once more on the front of the jersey, but this time on the right-hand side, while the manufacturer's logo (still Le Coq Sportif) was put on each sleeve.

In 1974, Merckx took his fifth Tour de France and the yellow jersey changed slightly, with the initials returning to the left-hand side and the sponsor of the jersey, Miko, switching to the right. It is understandable that such details probably went unnoticed by the Belgian champion, who was in excellent shape at the Brest start and won the prologue amid full Brittany fervor. The Tour then made a quick excursion into Great Britain, with Merckx passing the golden torch to his loyal teammate, Joseph Bruyère, for a few days.

When the Tour reached Gaillard, the end of the ninth stage, no one thought that anything else of any great significance could happen. Patrick Sercu had secured

The summit of Mont Ventoux stands at the end of the road. Merckx accelerates, unreachable in the summer light.

the green jersey, but from the fifth stage onward, Saint-Malo to Caen, Merckx was juggling with the golden shirt. The two Belgian champions thus made a pact. Childhood friends, and teammates for six-day races in the winter, they worked wonderfully together to neutralize the boisterous Gerben Karstens, holder of the yellow jersey at Dieppe, but who lost it to Sercu at Harelbeke. The Dutchman was on home territory though and took it back during the team time trial the next day.

Karstens continued to frustrate the plans of the two friends and their confrontation was bitterly fought out in close sprints, particularly at the various "hot spots", where bonus points were up for grabs, and by perilous shoulder-to-shoulder scraps at the finishes. The whole affair even took an acute turn on the finishing circuit at Châlons-sur-Marne where the Dutchman was the victim of a puncture. Merckx saw it all, stood up on the pedals and zoomed off to take the yellow jersey while Sercu, who could have won both the stage and yellow jersey, adopted a "wait-and-see" policy.

Karstens would never find the yellow jersey again. A curious eccentric, this man from the Netherlands had received a most bourgeois education from a lawyer father in Leiden, who had mapped out his career for him. But Karstens, who had become an agricultural engineer, wanted to go into agriculture. In conflict with his family, he found himself suddenly penniless and so became a professional cyclist—which just goes to show how far a bicycle can take you.

In this 1974 Tour, Merckx crushed the opposition in the Alps, even if he buckled under the Poulidor's acceleration during the ultra-steep ascent of the Mont du Chat during the tenth stage from Gaillard to Aix-les-Bains. At the summit, he was more than a minute behind the man from Limousin but caught up with him on the descent and beat him in the sprint.

Overall, however, Merckx suffered some tough times in the mountains, as the Pyrenees would prove, but he remained a fabulous competitor in all other aspects of the race. This would be his fifth and last victory in the Tour.

Even though he conceded to Bernard Thévenet the following year, he still wore the yellow jersey for ten days before handing it over to the Burgundian. The Nice to Praloup stage marked the twilight of his reign.

Eddy Merckx became "Mr." Merckx. The only Tour de France that he really lost still bore him a victory, a victory that he won over himself. It also was doubtless the most beautiful since it was the most difficult and the most painful.

Leading Lights

Philippe Thys, the first-ever triple winner

Philippe Thys, the link between two generations, that of the pre-war and that of the post-war

Opposite: Thys, the first ever cyclist to win three Tours de France (1913, 1914 and 1920). His third victory saw his team win twelve of the fifteen stages.

Previous spread: Anquetil (top-left), Bobet (top-right), Coppi (center), Hinault (bottom-left) and Indurain (bottom-right). Together they represent 20 Tours de France.

Philippe Thys wins his first Tour victory (1913).

The Belgian Philippe Thys represents the link between two generations—the generation before World War I and the generation that came after.

Born in Anderlecht, he wore the colors of VC Levallois and spent part of his career in France. The champion of consistency, he won the last two pre-war tours of 1913 and 1914, then came back after the war to win in 1920. He thus wore the yellow jersey in only one Tour de France, that of 1920, where he showed an inescapable superiority throughout the race.

Every one of Thys's moves was thought out; he never made an impulsive decision and there was never a single pedal-stroke more nervous than another. He weighed exactly the same—152 pounds—at the end of the Tour de France as he did at the start. This unshakable consistency made him a long-standing champion, the ideal Tour cyclist. He won his third Tour when he was thirty, seven years after his first one.

In this year of 1920, the Belgians had staged an unbelievable takeover of the Grande Boucle, since the first seven cyclists in the general classification were all from Thys's team. This astounding triumph was not quite to the liking of the French. The best-placed Frenchman was Barthélemy, in eighth place, 6 hours behind the yellow jersey.

Out of 15 stages, the Belgians won 12. Lambot, who had much improved, took 2 of them and proved himself the master of the Pyrenees. Thys, for his part, took three stage victories, in Nice, Strasbourg and Metz, with Sciur, Rossius, Heusghem and Mottiat (the first yellow jersey after the initial Paris to Le Havre stage) sharing the others between them. Apart from the stage victories, the Belgians swapped the yellow jersey between them. From Mottiat to Thys, three others took their turns to wear the shirt: Goethals, Rossius and Masson.

So what was Philippe Thys like, this austere citizen of Anderlecht, near Brussels, where he was born in 1890? According to the journalist Roger Bastide, he was of medium height, but with a compact figure; he sat low on the bike, a

225 yellow jerseys

(by the end of the 2000 Tour)

96 days : E. Merckx.

77 days : B. Hinault.

60 days : M. Indurain.

51 days : J. Anquetil.

39 days : A. Magne.

37 days : N. Frantz.

35 days : A. Leducq.

34 days : L. Bobet, O. Bottecchia.

27 days : L. Armstrong.

26 days : R. Maës, S. Maës, R. Vietto.

22 days : L. Fignon, G. LeMond, J. Zoetemelk.

20 days : G. Bartali.

19 days : F. Coppi, A. Darrigade, F. Gimondi.

18 days : R. Altig, M. Dewaele, J. Ullrich.

17 days : L. Ocaña, R. Pingeon.

16 days : B. Thévenet.

15 days : P. Delgado, D. Thurau.

14 days : S. Bauer, C. Nencini, B. Riis, L. Scieur, P. Thys.

13 days : M. Archambaud, G. Speicher.

12 days : V. Barteau, F. Kübler, A. Rolland, G. Vandenberghe, L. Van Impe, W. Wagtmans.

11 days : J. Bruyère, G. Desmet, H. Koblet.

10 days : K. Andersen, P. Lino.

9 days : P. Anderson, G. Groussard, F. Maertens, F. Magni.

8 days : L. Buysse, C. Chiappucci, G. Knetemann, R. Pevenage, R. Walkowiak.

7 days : J. Adriaenssens, F. Bahamontes, E. Christophe, B. Gauthier, L. Guerra, C. Guimard, E. Maechler, T. Marie, J. Planckaert, P. Simon, G. Van Slembrouk, H. Van Springel.

6 days : L. Aimar, C. Boardman, R. Cazala, M. Cipollini, V. Favero, J. Kirsipuu, R. Lévêque, J. Majerus, J. Marinelli, F. Moser, C. Mottet, M. Pantani, H. Pélissier, F. Schaër, F. Vervaecke.

5 days : J. Alavoine, E. Bautz, A. Benoît, K.H. Kunde, F. Lambot, J. Malléjac, J. Museeuw, J. Pedersen, F. Pélissier, B. Van de Kerkhove, E. Vanderaerden, C. Vasseur.

4 days : G. Bauvin, J. Catieau, A. Da Silva, R. Di Paco, A. Elli, S. Elliott, R. Géminiani, R. Hassenforder, J. Hoevenaers, R. Jacquinot, L. Jalabert, R. Lapébie, N. Laurédi, H. Martin, L. Mottiat, E. Pauwels, R. Sörensen, W. Van Est, G. Voorting, I. Zilioli, A. Zülle.

3 days : J. Diederich, J. Goldschmidt, C. Grosskost, S. Heulot, R. Lambrecht, G. Lemaire, E. Masson, D. Millar, W. Nelissen, J. Nijdam, O'Grady, C. Pélissier, R. Privat, J. Raas, S. Roche, W. Schroeders, J. Stevens, T. Van Vliet, M. Vermeulin.

2 days : H. Anglade, R. Bellenger, P. Brambilla, J. Buysse, R. Delisle, L. Desbiens, A. Dossche, J. Durand, V. Fontan, J. Fontenay, J. Forestier, C. Gaul, M. Gayant, A. Geldermans, I. Gotti, J. Hanegraaf, J. Janssen, G. Karstens, L. Peeters, R. Pensec, L. Piasecki, J. Robic, A. Ronconi, J. Rossius, W. Sels, K.P. Thaler, J. Van der Velde, R. Van Steenbergen, P. Vanzella, R. Wolfshohl.

1 day : J. Aerts, N. Barone, J.-F. Bernard, J.-R. Bernaudeau, Y. Bertin, E. Berzin, S. Biagioni, M. Bidot, J. Bossis, E. Breukink, J. Bruyneel, M. Bulla, N. Callens, A. Carrea, A. Deolet, M. Dussault, P. Egli, J. Engels, J.M. Errandonea, A. Fournier, D. Gaigne, J.-L. Gauthier, J.-P. Genet, F. Goethals, J. Groussard, B. Hamburger, A. Hamerlinck, H. Heusghem, S. Kelly, M. Kint, J.-C. Lebaube, L. Leblanc, L. Le Calvez, F. Le Drogo, D. Letort, H. Lubberding, F. Mahé, A. Mersch, F. Moncassin, W. Oberbeck, M. Poblet, G. Polidori, T. de Pra, G. Rebry, R. Riotte, G. Rossi, G. San Miguel, J. Schepens, P. Sercu, T. Simpson, J. Spruyt, A. Stieda, K. Stoepel, W. Teirlinck, A. Van der Poel, R. Van Looy, W. Van Neste, R. Virenque, R. Wagtmans, S. Yates, E. Zabel.

---

position which earned him his nickname "The Basset." He was a cantakerous calculator, and thin-skinned, quick to suspect any plot schemed against him. Not in the least interested in spectacular, but gratuitous, crowd-pleasing displays, he was one of those riders who obstinately kept up with every tempo, patiently observing and waiting for his rival to make a mistake.

In the 1920 Tour, none of his rivals were a match for him. His worst finish in a stage was fifth place, and he never stopped widening his lead. The Belgians maneuvered between themselves.

The Parc des Princes in Paris welcomed Thys as a triumphant victor, as reported by all of the press and particularly *L'Auto,* which wrote: "Philippe Thys took his lap of honor, to the thunderous acclaim of the crowd, while the band played *La Brabançonne* and the spectators invaded the track. The conqueror was obliged to finish his victory parade on foot. Submerged by a veritable human sea, he only just made it to the registration table, to sign in, and the security personnel had great difficulty in extracting him from the hugs and kisses of his admirers so that he could finally greet his family."

The Pélissier and Bottecchia revelation

After the war, the Tour de France was able to find a true nationwide equilibrium. The great race finally included stages on its new eastern frontier, and thrust ever deeper into the mountain ranges, progressively getting nearer to the various borders.

Some strong characters appeared in the peloton, particularly Frenchman Henri Pélissier and his brother Francis.

Henri had already asserted himself before the war with his friend Lucien Petit-Breton, victor of the Tour de France in 1907 and 1908. In Italy, Henri Pélissier had won Milan-San Remo, then Bordeaux-Paris and Paris-Roubaix, in particular, but as for the Tour de France, the previous years seemed to prove that he was not a "man of the Tour." Incidentally, his caprices were legendary. In 1912, for example, he refused to take part in the race to protest the standard ration of food that they were trying to impose on the riders.

Nevertheless, the public held him in very high esteem, an esteem that Henri Desgrange rather mistrusted. He knew that a man with such an intransigent and violent character is capable of not only the best but also the worst. This explains why their relationship was rather less than cordial. The following exchange between them, a few days before Paris-Roubaix, is proof of this: "Don't forget," Desgrange snapped at him, "that it was *L'Auto* that made you!"

"Never!" retorted Henri. "It was I who made *L'Auto!*

Next Sunday you will print: First, Henri Pélissier, then you will see the difference in your sales between this name and the others!"

Sure enough, the following Sunday, Henri Pélissier won Paris-Roubaix.

Finally, he set his heart on the Tour de France in 1923, but no one really believed he could do it. His Automoto team had hired an unknown, withdrawn and taciturn Italian, Ottavio Bottecchia, on the pretext that he might serve as a backup leader. The bicycle manufacturer was motivated by commercial reasons and at first decided to hire four Italian cyclists. With the deal worked out by correspondence, the journalist Fabio Orlandini was given the responsibility of swiftly wrapping up the deal. However, only one Italian cyclist actually showed up in Paris, and that was Bottecchia. A disappointed Mr. Montet, president of Automoto bicycles, wanted to send him home, but Pierrard, the directeur sportif, disagreed, arguing that since this plucky lad had taken the pains to make the journey, they might as well use him. So this was how Ottavio Bottecchia made his debut in the Tour de France.

Everyone soon saw that Automoto's choice had not been in vain. Bottecchia took the second-place sprint on the first stage and then won the second stage from Le Havre to Cherbourg, taking over the yellow jersey. After losing it in Sables d'Olonne, he took it back in the Pyrenees, on the mountain stage between the Bayonne and Luchon.

For the time being, Henri Pélissier kept his composure, content to base his own race on that of Bottecchia and bide his time. The moment came on the Col d'Allos, on the Nice to Briançon stage. During the climb, he bridged to the leading group, consisting of Buysse, Alancourt, Alavoine and

A fast sprinter, Bottecchia also proved to be
a remarkable climber, capable of taking
a 12-minute lead all on his own, over the Tourmalet,
as he did in 1924.

The enigmatic Bottecchia. Withdrawn and taciturn,
he surfaced mysteriously in the Tour de France
and immediately took second place. It was the start
of great things.

Bottecchia. The extremely fast pace soon proved to be fatal for Bottecchia who was using too large a gear ratio. Pélissier saw that he was in trouble and so made a powerful attack. He soon found himself out on his own. On the descent he let Buysse and Alavoine catch up with him, climbed the Col de Vars alongside them and then attacked the Izoard. Clearly fixed on his goal and with remarkable ease, Peelissier broke away again, and once more found himself alone and, with amazing ease, set off toward triumph. Even Henri Desgrange, in *L'Auto,* felt obliged to use epithets that he would perhaps have preferred to forget.

"Twice he got off to drink some water," commented the patron of the Tour, "but all done calmly and without haste, like someone who knows what they're doing. And the huge mountain seemed to bend itself, to diminish under the victorious thrusting of his muscles. More than twenty times, on the harshest slopes, with his hands on top of the handlebars, he looked back down at the bottom of the valley and the twists of the interminable road, with the look of an eagle surveying its prey. His eyes scoured the depths of the abyss for a sign of Bottecchia's yellow jersey, but the truth was that today it was the greyhound that had beaten the heavyset men like Lambot, Scieur and Heusghem, whom we had always thought of as the typical Tour de France rider."

But that was not all. Whatever his personal feelings for this strong-headed rider, Desgrange showed by these comments that he admired the valor of the man and the superiority of his mind.

"Henri Pélissier," he continued, "has put on a show for us that is the equal of the highest artistic performance. His victory has the wonderful organization and classicism of the works of Racine, the beauty of a perfect statue, a faultless painting or a piece of music destined to stay in our memory for evermore. You may consider this victory from any angle you like, but you will not find a single flaw nor any dubious aspect to it. It was beautifully developed, a sporting opus that will remain inscribed forever in the annals of our Tour de France."

After another breakaway on the Col du Galibier, Henri Pélissier won the Tour with a half-hour lead on Bottecchia.

The destiny of the "Mason of Friuli"

Taciturn, keeping to himself and away from all the hubbub, Bottecchia was capable of prevailing in the mountains, on the flat, and in the sprints. Henri Pélissier had to call on all his skill in order to confront him. He recognized that: "Bottecchia has the look of a wild peasant, but on a bike, hats off

Sixth stage of the 1924 Tour. Ottavio Bottecchia in the Tourmalet. He won the stage with an 18-minute lead over the Belgian Buysse. He became a legend, wearing the yellow jersey from the first day to the last.

to him, what style! He seems made for the race. He is slim, lean, weather-beaten and with a face like the blade of a knife. Arms and legs that never end. I doubt that anyone ever taught him anything when he started, but he sits well on the bike. And that's class. He must be at least 29 but muscularly he's as good as new."

In 1924, free of any team duty after the withdrawal of Henri Pélissier, Bottecchia won the Tour "with one leg" as they say, taking the yellow jersey the first day and wearing it right until the end. Just a detail though; there was one stage in which he didn't wear the yellow jersey, and that was from Toulon to Nice. This was because the political ideas that he espoused were not exactly in line with those of the Italian government at the time. So fearing that he might be attacked by fanatics arriving from nearby Italy, he gave up the famous shirt for this Riviera stage and wore a purple one instead; less glorious perhaps, but also less visible.

He opened up some impressive time gaps in the Pyrenees and finally triumphed with a 35-minute lead over the second-place man, Nicolas Frantz—who had managed to hold him in check in the Alps, as did Giovanni Brunero, the three-times winner of the Tour of Italy, who took the Nice to Briançon stage.

Bottecchia thus brought Italy its first victory in the Tour de France.

During his journey home by train, the ex-"Mason of Friuli" could not bear to put his yellow jersey in his suitcase. He wore it under his jacket, treasured, for the whole journey.

He returned to the Tour de France in 1925, although he was not quite so dominating. Winner of the first stage, the yellow jersey was taken from him by an awfully aggressive Belgian, Adelin Benoît, who kept it until Bayonne, at the end of the seventh stage, where Bottecchia took it back from him.

But Benoît had not had his last word. During the Bayonne to Luchon stage, he went in hot pursuit of his lost trophy. But it was only an intermission, since, in Perpignan, where Frantz won the stage, Benoît had knee problems and lost 46 minutes. The yellow jersey was once more on Bottecchia's back and the trophy stayed there for the rest of the race. The Italian won the Tour by 54 minutes, over his teammate Lucien Buysse.

On June 2, 1927, Bottecchia met a tragic end. He was found unconscious after having gone out for a solitary training ride. He died a few days later in the Gemona hospital, caused by a fracture to the base of his skull.

The two "greats" of the 1924 Tour. Bottecchia (left), Frantz (right).

Frantz climbing fiercely through the Pyrenees passes in the stage from Bayonne to Luchon in the 1927 Tour. Winner in Luchon, he took the yellow jersey and never let it go.

Several versions of his dramatic death were circulated including one in which Bottecchia was killed with a rock thrown by a peasant who had surprised him picking grapes in his vineyard. Perhaps he simply had a touch of sunstroke, causing him to fall. The mystery remains.

Nicolas Frantz, "the Methodical"

At the start of the 1927 Tour de France, Henri Desgrange made an innovation. To avoid long promenades on the flat stages and to give the race a permanent vigor, he instituted separate starts, by team; in effect, team time trials. This idea didn't suit everyone, but it is true that the race immediately got tougher. Francis Pélissier pulled on the first yellow jersey in Dieppe, at the head of his Dilecta team. The race still ran in a counter-clockwise direction, but the Tour discovered new sites and new stage towns, since, for the first time, the race now consisted of twenty-four stages, instead of the initial fifteen and then seventeen.

Francis Pélissier withdrew during the sixth stage from Dinan to Brest, after falling ill, and the yellow jersey was handed to his teammate, the French champion Ferdinand Le Drogo. In the heart of his native Brittany, the young Ferdinand, feeling like a superhero, left his teammates behind and tired himself out in a solitary struggle. He would later withdraw on the eighth stage, in Sables d'Olonne, leaving the yellow tunic with the Belgian Hector Martin, who would wear it until the Pyrenees, where Nicolas Frantz from Luxembourg broke away.

28 years old, Frantz showed all the characteristics of an all-around cyclist. It is impossible to imagine the care, attention to detail and application with which the citizen of the grand-duchy took part in the Tour. Bordeaux-Paris, Paris-Tours or Paris-Roubaix meant nothing to him! Only the Grande Boucle counted for him, and he focused on it entirely. Perfectly lucid during the race and impassive off the bike, his one fault was an alleged fussiness. Nevertheless one has to agree: Frantz never complained about anything. He was just scrupulously detailed. At the start of the Tour, he went so far as to take twenty-four jerseys, twenty-four pairs of socks and twenty-four pairs of leggings with him, one for each day of the race.

Although it must be said that Frantz did not represent the exceptional athlete par excellence, it would be difficult to find another sportsman who practiced his craft with such strictness, or even with such love. He stored up energy reserves like one stashes away savings. A discreet man, he remains the champion of technique.

During the rest day in Bayonne, the day before he

took the yellow jersey at Luchon, Frantz's roommate André Leducq, related: "I came back from a little afternoon ride, and Nicolas, always a hermit, was meditatively considering a panoply of objects neatly arranged on the table: two sweaters, two pairs of leg-warmers, woolen gloves and…a flashlight! I asked him what this was all for and he answered me in his austere way: "You can't see clearly up there…and it's cold, very cold!"

The preparations must have worked, for Frantz won the next stage, put the yellow jersey on and was no longer troubled.

In 1928 he completed the double. He asserted his superiority from the very first stage, when at the head of the powerful Alcyon team, he took the yellow jersey, never to relinquish it.

He experienced only one moment of panic in this Tour. The scene took place during the nineteenth stage from Metz to Charleville, a stage that promised to be singularly uneventful. The yellow jersey had a lead of more than an hour and a solid team. He looked forward to the last three stages with a certain pleasure. But 1¼ miles before Longuyon, he and his teammates had a big fright. While crossing a railroad, Frantz suddenly saw his bike collapse beneath him. The confusion in the Alcyon team camp was indescribable. The driver of the directeur sportif's car wanted to take Frantz to an Alcyon retailer, so that he could continue with a brand new bike. The offence would have cost him an hour's penalty! Luckily directeur sportif Ludovic Feuillet was able to procure a borrowed bike for him, complete with mudguards, red lights and…a girl's frame.

Mounting this contraption, he reached Charleville 28 minutes behind teammate Leducq, who was lying second overall, covering the remaining 60 miles at more than 16½ mph. The Tour was won.

He thus became the second man in history to wear the yellow jersey from the first to the last stage.

The new way with André Leducq

The 1930 Tour de France marked a turning point for the race with the establishment of national teams; all of the cyclists mounted bicycles in the identical enameled yellow, the color of *L'Auto.*

The decision to do this was not without courage, since the French bike manufacturers, big advertisers in *L'Auto,* could, as a reprisal, withdraw their advertising. If this happened, then how would it have been possible to fund all of the cyclists, pay

Frantz took his second consecutive Tour de France in 1928. He took the last stage, too, just to ensure his superiority.

A reserved and observant man, Nicolas Frantz was the champion of technique. It was said of him that he didn't neglect a single detail and that "he accumulated energy reserves like some people accumulate savings."

André Leducq: powerful, sturdy, an excellent cyclist. The ever-smiling champion won two Tours de France and twenty-four stages. Author of as many underhand tricks as he was of great exploits.

Confidence and serenity were Leducq's major assets…and the reward was often rather pleasant!

for their supplies and all of their equipment, the hiring of all the staff, board, lodging and transport for this merry band?

In order to finance the whole shebang, the organizer came up with a great idea: the invention of the publicity caravan.

The year 1930 hailed a renewal of French cycling. Jean Maréchal had made his name in the one-day classics and Charles Pélissier, third brother in the clan, was shooting up through the ranks like an arrow. A member of the French team, Pélissier won the first stage of the Tour from Paris to Caen and took over the yellow jersey, but why was it that seven years after the success of his older brother, he couldn't personally win this great race? After all, he proved himself to be the great master of the flat stages, winning eight stages in total and finishing second seven times.

But as soon as the mountains appeared, his teammate André Leducq went into action in the first Pyrenees stage. Leducq possessed everything of the popular hero: talent, courage and the humble destiny of a kid from Saint-Ouen. Additionally, he was surrounded by a proud French team, full of buddies who were no longer each fighting for their own bicycle manufacturer, but together for a French victory.

Six men stood guard until Fontan and Mauclair were forced to quit, lessening the protection of Leducq and his yellow jersey, which was coveted by the Italian Learco Guerra and the Belgian Jef Demuysère. At the foot of the Alps, the Frenchman's victory seemed complete, but he still had to reckon with the hazards of the ever-treacherous mountains.

To start with, Leducq broke a pedal during the descent of the Galibier. He repaired it thanks to the help of a spectator cyclist. He had only just remounted his bike when he saw a hurricane streak past him: Guerra. This Italian was a dangerous man, an energetic and efficient rider, with powerful back muscles that enabled him to accelerate strongly and create big time differences. Leducq set off in hot pursuit and was clearly faster than the Italian, but he seemed to have confused speed with haste. He took a graveled bend at 45 mph, skidded, flipped three times and came to rest just a few centimeters from the edge of the ravine, stunned, with his knee cut open and bleeding profusely. A few of his comrades were close at hand, notably Antonin Magne and his brother Pierre. Leducq's knee had become one huge laceration, which became a vast black clot of coagulated blood. He looked at his beautiful yellow jersey and burst into tears. Later, he would recount how at that moment he had the awful impression that his jersey had changed color, and that the yellow tunic that he wore had turned into a gray rag, like in the fairy tale where Cinderella turns back into a mucky peasant girl once morning comes. "A dream faded, one that had been pursued for so many years: victory in the most wonderful race in the world," wrote André Chassaignon and André Poirier in their history of the Tour de France.

The whole of the French team soon surrounded their Dédé. Charles Pélissier took command: "You don't give up when you've got the yellow jersey to take care of," he proclaimed. "Are you listening to me, Dédé? We're all going to go flat out; you'll stick with us and we'll take you up to Guerra."

"There's also Demuysère," murmured Leducq.

"Demuysère is an old nag," interrupted Bidot, a little exasperated. "Come on, get on the saddle! I've had enough of seeing you blubbering like that! You're not a woman after all! Let's have a look at your knee! Stretch out your leg…now bend it…there's nothing broken. Let's go then, you'll warm up on the way!"

Faced with this torrent of orders, Leducq stood up and got back on the road, escorted by his teammates. The valley road was in sight and Charles Pélissier set a hellish pace. Leducq clenched his teeth. He had lost about a quarter of an hour on the Italian. Overall, Guerra was just 16:13 behind!

Near Saint-Jean-de-Maurienne, the French team caught up with a few dispersed riders. They were now twenty-odd, relaying themselves through the valley. Ahead, Guerra and Demuysère could only count on the help of the little Spaniard Trueba.

"Go on Charlot, go on Dédé!"

The crowd encouraged the united colors of red, white and blue riding strongly in tight formation.

After 45 miles of pursuit, Leducq and his fellow warriors finally saw Guerra and Demuysère. As they raced through Albertville, the yellow jersey was saved. The leading group, now thirty strong, headed for Evian. The French team was not finished though. It had to win the stage, because a bonus minute would be awarded to the winner. Charles Pélissier launched the sprint for the yellow jersey, avoided Belgian Aimé Dossche, who was considered dangerous, and let Leducq cross the finish line first.

It would be useless to describe the atmosphere within this French team, that had just made a collective demonstration of its strength and, so would go on to win the Tour de France, while Pélissier would win the last four stages.

The wonderful French sequel

The solidarity of the members of the French team was confirmed once more during the 1931 Tour de France,

Method, will power and professional conscience were the hallmarks of Antonin Magne, who defined the secret of the Tour thus: "You have to know how to last, to save your energy, so that you're as strong at the end as you were at the start."

THE GREAT FRENCH TEAMS OF THE 1930'S.

Above, 1936: (left to right) Cloarec, Gamard, Speicher, Le Grèves, Chocque, Marcaillou, Tanneveau, Thietard, Lapébie and Archambaud.

Below, 1933: rest day in Evian. We can recognize Leducq, Le Grèves, Lapébie, Le Calvez, Archambaud, Magne and Speicher.

won by Antonin Magne. "Tonin," a courageous man from Ytrac in the Cantal blessed with tremendous willpower, forced himself each morning, whatever the weather, to move a large boulder at the bottom of his garden so as to toughen himself up for the kind of difficult and tedious tasks that a champion worthy of the name should never shun.

The crux of the 1931 Tour lay once more in the Pyrenees. The Belgians Schepers and Dewaele proved themselves the best on the Aubisque and Tourmalet passes, but they fell victim to punctures and had to concede the stage victory to Magne, who arrived in Luchon with a 4:42 lead over the Italian revelation Antonio Pesenti and took the yellow jersey. He never relinquished it.

In the Alps, the same Pesenti gave Magne a few problems. He came within several minutes of him, while Demuysère took 2 minutes off him up the Col d'Allos. Magne hung on though, supported remarkably by his teammate Charles Pélissier, who seeing his leader in difficulty brought him up to the front.

Although there were only two stages left until the finish in the Parc des Princes, Magne kept on repeating: "The Tour is not won until the last turn of the pedal." His anxiety was casting a shadow on his hopes. The man from Auvergne was at the end of his tether, and his teammates were too.

In his room, Magne glanced across at Leducq, stretched out on his bed and sleeping like a baby: "If only I had your constitution," thought Tonin. "Only two days left if nothing happens to me! If I crack, then the Belgians will pull all the stops out…Come on, got to sleep."

But the yellow jersey just couldn't drop off. He tossed and turned on his bed and his stirring eventually woke his friend Dédé.

"If you can't sleep," the latter said to him, "then just read for a bit, you'll see it'll make you drowsy. Look at all that stack of letters on the table. You've got some lady admirers there…"

And Leducq burst out laughing, an infectious laugh that soon had Tonin tearing open the letters.

"Look what they've written to me Dédé, "the yellow jersey suddenly cried out.

On a simple sheet of school paper, an anonymous Belgian had written these simple words: "Mr. Antonin Magne, I am writing to warn you that Rebry has written to his mother saying he'll mount a big attack with Demuysère on the stage from Charleville to Malo-les-Bains. Best wishes."

Leducq thought it was a joke, and Magne didn't believe the hoax. The letter came from Gaston Rebry's village, on the border.

"There's only one thing to do," concluded Leducq. "Tomorrow, we stick to both Rebry and Demuysère like glue and if they try anything then we respond."

And so the two men went back to sleep.

The next day, the sky was swept by heavy clouds. Wind and rain were predicted for the stage. Magne had discreetly warned his comrades in the French team of the dastardly plans of the men from Flanders.

The yellow jersey, far from reassured, put on his black shoes and looked at Rebry, nicknamed "the Bulldog." If he had chosen this stage then it was not in vain. It was a route of cobblestones par excellence and Rebry loved this kind of course. Had he not won Paris-Roubaix a few months earlier on these very same roads? Magne then looked at Demuysère, a force of nature in the same vein as Rebry. He had first come to light in a Bordeaux-Paris race where he had finished with a cheek lacerated by a flying pedal.

And so the 170-mile stage began. Magne would have to wait a little less than 60 miles for the predicted attack. The two Belgians launched their offensive on a cobblestone bend. The yellow jersey lost 10 meters. Leducq saw what was afoot and sounded the alarm. Magne did react very quickly, however. With a big effort he got on their wheels. But the Belgians just increased their pace. One by one the men in the leading group fell back, asphyxiated by the crazy pace. Rebry and Demuysère relayed each other like demons. Magne hung on, lost contact, came back, lost another 10 meters, came back…and then crashed. But his bike was intact and Magne set off again and caught up with his two demons.

The trio reached the finish 17 minutes ahead of the first chasers. Rebry won the sprint, with Magne placing second. He had cinched the Tour de France, but what a fright!

French cycling had reached a summit. The following year, Leducq again found victory. He picked up the yellow jersey on the third stage and never let it go.

The French team served as an example to all. In fact, in 1933, it gathered together the greatest characters of the prewar years: Archambaud, Le Calvez, Pélissier, Magne, Le Grevès, Lapébie and Speicher. It was Georges Speicher who won this twenty-seventh Tour de France, after a lightning climb to fame. In two years, he had acquired international status. And this year, he once more triumphed in the world championship.

During the Tour de France, he engaged in an intimate struggle with his teammate Maurice Archambaud. The

The picture that moved the whole of France in 1934. Worry and despair are etched across René Vietto's face, after having given his wheel to his team leader, the yellow jersey, Antonin Magne. A legend has just been born.

Georges Speicher, winner of the 1933 Tour de France. It was a triumph of good health, great humor and perfect consistency.

At the 1939 Tour, René Vietto's glorious dream crumbled on the Izoard and he ceded his yellow jersey to Sylvère Maës (right). Between them stands the actor Albert Préjean who had come to congratulate them at the Parc de Princes.

two Frenchmen took the yellow jersey in turn for the first 12 stages …while remaining the best of friends. The unity of the national team would remain unbroken.

Winner of the stage from Grenoble to Gap, after a fantastic battle, leader in Marseille after his climb in the Alps, Speicher struggled on the Tourmalet, picked up in the Aubisque and, thanks to his downhill skills, consolidated his position. On the way out of the Pyrenees his success was assured.

The elegant silhouette of Speicher, with his long and slim limbs gave him the air of a wader bird. He was an unconditional fan of the derailleur, an accessory still fought against, for reasons of economy, by the majority of bicycle manufacturers. Although the derailleur was still not allowed in the 1933 Tour, he invented a special assembly for the rear-brake stirrup that would make the braking more sensitive and progressive.

Beneath his apparent dilettantism, Georges Speicher was a realistic and observant technician.

In 1934, the French team continued to clean up and Magne seized victory again. The darling of that year's Tour was René Vietto, a young man from Cannes, just twenty years old. Enlisted by the French team, he had won his stripes a few weeks before in the Wolber Grand Prix, a stage race considered as the crucible for young talents. Vietto won it and headed for glory.

In this year of 1934, this ex-bellboy of the Majestic and Palm Beach hotels in Cannes soon showed his amazing climbing qualities. He dueled with the Italian Giuseppe Martano in the Alps, but the latter became particularly dangerous in the general classification for the French team's leader, Magne, yellow jersey since the finish of the second stage in Charleville.

The French team dominated the race outrageously. But they had to remain vigilant. When the race reached the foot of the Pyrenees from Perpignan to Ax-les-Thermes, everyone expected a fresh dual between Magne and Martano, particularly on the Col de Puymorens. What would Vietto do? Would he respect the team spirit? Could he hold back his youthful ardor? In the end, he broke away and reached the summit of the Col de Puymorens in the lead. They all regrouped, but Magne missed a bend on the descent and found himself thrown to the ground. His bike took a pounding and the front wheel was wrecked. Martano saw this and accelerated. Lapébie reacted swiftly, alerted Vietto and shouted to him to give his wheel to his team leader. The young man from Cannes did as he was told with his heart aching.

The next day, on the stage from Ax-les-Thermes to Luchon, the scenario repeated itself. Magne suffered another fall on the descent of the Col du Portet-d'Aspet and Vietto was obliged to sacrifice not just a wheel, but his whole bike.

So Magne won another Tour. Ever the dominator, he proved his class once more in the tenth stage from Luchon to Tarbes, by vigorously attacking the Italian Martano from the very start. It was the coup de grâce.

Sylvère Maës's double

The 1936 Tour de France started under a veritable deluge. The rainstorms lasted for seven days, during which the yellow jersey played musical chairs. The garment was first of all borne by the Swiss Paul Egli, in Lille, before passing it to Maurice Archambaud, the winner in Charleville. He had hardly taken possession of it before it was whisked away by Arsène Mersch from Luxembourg. Most irritated by this, Archambaud gathered all his energy, won the Ballon d'Alsace stage, in Belfort, and took back the leader's trophy. But "the Dwarf," as he was nicknamed, complained of a chill and there was a degree of uncertainty as to how much longer he would remain in yellow.

At the same time, in Charleville, Henri Desgrange, who had undergone an operation at the start of the Tour and had nevertheless insisted on carrying out his official duties, was obliged to hand over the director's reins to Jacques Goddet, the most competent to take on this great task. A page was turned in the history of the Tour.

During the eighth stage from Grenoble to Briançon, which was won by the Breton Jean-Marie Goasmat, the Belgian Sylvère Maës went into action. Archambaud crumbled and the Belgian team received the recompense for their long and commendable efforts.

Was the Tour already over? Everyone feared so. Antonin Magne, who was 1:35 behind Maës, was called upon to blast back. He resolutely attacked the yellow jersey during the stage from Briançon to Digne and put some distance between him and Maës, who suffered an unfortunate puncture. But Maës had an elite team and, with his so-called Black Guard, came fighting back on the descent of the Col d'Allos.

And so the rest of this Tour de France would be run under the aegis of Magne and the Flemish: a solid and conscientious work, but hardly exciting.

Sylvère Maës proved his incontestable superiority. Industrious and casual at the same time, and of an optimism bordering on recklessness, he never gave the impression of really getting down to work.

After a turbulent episode in the 1937 Tour, Sylvère

Floods at the 1936 Tour: a violent storm hit the race during the first stage from Paris to Lille. Maurice Archambaud and the Swiss Paul Egli attempt to find their way to Carvin along the flooded road. Egli would win in Lille and take the first yellow jersey of the Tour.

In the 1936 Tour, Magne, (foreground) couldn't shake off Sylvère Maës, next to him. The Belgian's victory was well forecast and Magne seems resigned to it.

Maës returned victoriously to the Grande Boucle in 1939, with great skill and perceptiveness.

The great novelty of the 1939 Tour was the creation of regional teams. Among other innovations was the increase in the number of time trials to five, with one of them in the mountains, from Bonneval to Bourg-Saint-Maurice, including the ascent of the Col de l'Iseran.

This Tour, which was terribly hard, tested many of the competitors to the limit. The regional teams attacked relentlessly, taking stages on their home ground: the Bretons Eloi Tassin and Pierre Cloarec in Rennes and Brest, the south-westerners Edmund Pagès and Raymond Passat in Royan and Bordeaux, and Fabien Galateau in Marseille.

This Tour was marked by the resurrection of the young man from Cannes, René Vietto, who had been out of the news since his memorable 1934 Tour, where he had sacrificed his chances for his leader Antonin Magne. Vietto took the leader's jersey in Lorient, at the end of the fourth stage, won by Raymond Louviot. Henceforth he set himself to defending this jersey with savage energy, and all of this before the mountains, to place himself out of reach of the Belgians, the strong favorites.

The racer from Cannes almost lost the jersey in Pau, but extended his lead the next day in stormy weather at the finish in Toulouse, after a fiery pursuit of the Belgian Edward Vissers. An ambitious rider, who insisted on asserting himself, contrary to the conventions of a team race, Vissers resolutely attacked, without bothering about Sylvère Maës, his leader. The two Flemish riders eyed each other scornfully after the finish in the city of Violets where Vissiers had just won the stage. From this moment on, everyone knew that the two teammates would no longer be able to live with each other.

Maës waited for the Alps to deal his death-blow. He suddenly attacked, 10 miles from the summit of the Izoard, taking everybody by surprise. His rivals looked at each other, flabbergasted, and only Pierre Gallien, who was the first to come to his senses, was able to catch up with the Belgian.

Vietto was irreparably left behind on this ascent, paying for his previous efforts. His pace was that of a man beaten, both physically and morally. The wonderful dream of the young man from Cannes had crumbled.

A marvel of equilibrium and perceptiveness, Maës took the yellow jersey at Briançon, and then consolidated his lead by beating Vietto by 10 minutes in the time trial over the Col de l'Iseran.

He had won the Tour for a second time.

Sylvère Maës, who was so often seen on the podium was also no stranger to adversity (Tour 1938).

Opposite: Maës was the typical Tour cyclist. He had neither amazing talent nor startling brilliance, but was a strong and steady man, ready to face any trial.

Maës never fell victim to uncertainty. He just produced the necessary effort at the required moment. This enabled him to win two Tours de France (1936 and 1939).

Gino Bartali during his first Tour de France (1937). An already total ascendancy that would be halted only by a stroke of bad luck.

Opposite: World War II (1939-1945) put an end to many careers. But Bartali emerged from the embers, winning the 1948 Tour, ten years after his first triumph. His faithful teammate Giovanni Corrieri stands next to him.

The authority of a true champion. Bartali remained blissfully ignorant of the customs and habits of "French-style" races. In the mountains he raised his level above everyone and so took his first yellow jersey (Tour de France 1937).

Henri Desgrange, Father of the Tour, between Bartali (yellow jersey) and his teammate Francesco Camusso. In 1938, the Tuscan won his first Tour. His freshness is startling.

Bartali, "Gino the Pious"

Bartali when facing some big decisions: serious and impenetrable.

H e was Tuscan, which means that he was born smart. And smart he was. But before this factory worker's son could taste the fruits of glory that victory might bring, even if it were just regional, he had to earn his bread. When he made a break-away with another rider, the latter would often confide: "My fiancée is waiting for me at the finish line. Let me win and I'll give you the winner's prize." Gino Bartali thus pocketed both the first and second prizes, which allowed his dad, Torello, to improve their everyday life.

Then Aldo Bini appeared on the scene, a sturdy Tuscan like him.

Bini was already known as the "God of Italy", but Bartali soon asserted himself and, in 1938, won the Tour de France. The war then robbed him of the best years of his career. But his skill was still intact. Ten years later he won a second Tour de France. Fausto Coppi, five years younger than him, had already shown his mettle by winning the Tour of Italy in 1940, although he was only supposed to be Bartali's water carrier.

An aggravated and pervasive rivalry was already dividing Italy into two opposing clans. Coppi, the rising star, slightly eclipsed Bartali and the latter was most piqued by it. Bartali's first encounter with the Tour de France and the yellow jersey was back in 1937. Paris was overrun by a crowd of foreigners who had come to visit the Universal Exhibition. Bartali was picked as one of the favorites, after his recent victory in the Tour of Italy, but everyone wondered how he would get through the first stages, which included the treacherous cobblestone roads of northern France. To everyone's amazement, he got through them without a scratch. Then came the famous Ballon d'Alsace, the first serious obstacle, which earned the Italian this revealing and promising phrase from Henri Desgrange: "I don't give a fig for the classification; I have never seen anything as wonderful as Bartali on the Ballon d'Alsace." In Grenoble, after having crossed the

Bartali would win the 1948 Tour de France and all Italy would again breathe freely. The country had been in a state of near revolution for several days, since the assassination attempt on the communist leader Palmiro Togliatti. Bartali gave the Italians a fresh identity. The sacred union was patched up and Italy was saved.

mighty Galibier in the lead, he won the stage and became race leader. But the Tour had not finished with its shocks, and neither had Bartali. Misfortune lay in wait for him twenty miles from the finish in Briançon. On a twisting descent, made slippery by the rain, the Florentine skidded, lost control of his bike and crashed into the balustrade of a rustic bridge that crossed a small tributary of the Durance River. He flew over the barrier and into the torrent, which luckily was not too deep. Seriously hurt, he got back on the road and made Briançon only 10 minutes behind the leaders, but managing to keep the yellow jersey. But his injuries were too much, and four days later, he withdrew.

Bartali returned the following year…and won. He showed his supremacy everywhere. In Briançon, the Italian supporters had crossed the border and, as they prepared to carry Bartali off in triumph, the president of the Italian Cycling Union held the crowd back, shouting: "Don't touch him. He's a god!" By the finish in Paris, the Italian rider had beaten the runner-up Félicien Belgian Vervaecke, by more than 18 minutes. A national fund was set up in Italy. Il Duce, Benito Mussolini, was the first to contribute.

Ten years later came his second victory in the Tour de France. Bartali was thirty-four years old and extremely apprehensive. He resolved to memorize the numbers of all the riders whom he didn't know, those who it seemed a good idea to keep an eye on. There were twenty of them.

A few miles from the start, the peloton was caught in a violent storm, and the raincoats hid the numbers that Bartali was watching. A stroke of pure luck put him on the wheel of the Belgian Brik Schotte, whom he already knew, having

Bartali the victor. He drew his strength from some deep mysticism. Raised in Italy to the rank of a divinity, he witnessed the crowds throwing themselves down to touch the ground he had cycled over with their forehead, and to kiss the dust thrown up by his wheels.

ridden with him in Belgium. Bartali hung on to him like a drowning man and beat him in the sprint to win the stage at the Trouville velodrome. Such was the story of his first yellow jersey in 1948, defying every prediction, including those of the Florentine himself. This Tour marked the arrival of Louison Bobet who took the yellow jersey in Nantes. He was still the leader in Lourdes, where the stage was won by Bartali who, very serenely, sent a telegram to the Pope asking for a special blessing for him and his teammates. After dinner, he made his way to the grotto and, kneeling, prayed to the Virgin Mary "Madonna," he said, "I have not come here to ask you to help me win, that I can do on my own; all I ask of you is not to let me fall."

As the Tour took a rest day in Cannes, a drama was unfolding in Italy. The leader of the Communist Party, Palmiro Togliatti, victim of an assassination attempt, was in a critical condition and the country feared major public disorder. The Italian prime minister, Alcide De Gasperi, called Bartali on the phone: "Things are very bad, so I would like to know one thing, Gino, do you think you can win the Tour?"

"I'm no magician," Gino replied. "The Tour finishes in Paris and there's still more than one week of the race to go."

"It's important, Gino, very important for Italy, and for everyone…"

The Tuscan finally understood. He was a hero in Italy, and if he won, he could draw the attention of his fellow countrymen and calm the atmosphere of revolt that was spreading through the land.

In the Alps, Bartali soared over his rivals. All admired the courage of Bobet, but he just wasn't up to it when faced with the Italian. Ten years after his first success, Bartali once more tasted victory.

In Italy, many people were enjoying their vacations, while Togliatti was slowly recovering from his injuries.

There was no more talk of revolution.

Gino Bartali thought that he had been guided by mystical forces. He ceaselessly called out his wishes to heaven, and prayed to God at the start, during the race, and at the finish. When the decisive moments were upon him, he called on his personal confessor Don Bruno, who had previously been blessing everything that he ate during the race. Bartali gave a lot of money to good causes and, during the war, helped the escape of Jews who were hidden in a convent in Assisi, by carrying documents on his bike from the Archbishop of Florence up to Umbria.

Tour de France 1951. Bartali was counting on the Izoard to mount a major attack, but Coppi caught him and went ahead to win in Briançon.

To honor the public, Bartali enters the Parc de Princes first, at the finish of the 1949 Tour, when he was beaten in the final classification by his rival Coppi.

And Coppi appeared...

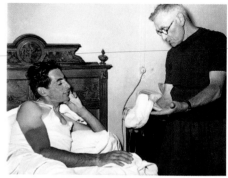

The "Campionissimo" sought perfection even balancing of his diet, with a particular menu for a particular moment...

Covered with honors and hit by many a stroke of fate, Coppi would give cycling a prodigious leap forward.

Opposite: Brothers in arms, Coppi passes his water bottle to Bartali in the Tourmalet. They joined forces in the search for victory, although their compatriot Fiorenzo Magni, the yellow jersey, was unable to accompany them this time. Here the only man who could keep up with the prestigious duo was "Apo" Lazarides (Tour de France 1949).

The 1949 Tour has just finished. Coppi puts on the winner's emblem for the last time, watched by the final day's winner, Rik Van Steenbergen.

Fausto Coppi had already seen enormous glory. He had just won the Tour of Italy as if it was simply a formality. He was urged to take part in the Tour de France, but numerous problems had to be resolved first, since his participation was linked to the nonselection of Bartali. Coppi reproached the Tuscan's lack of team spirit.

Several meetings had to be held, before the sacred union was made, and the pact sealed in Chiavari by official deed.

The Tour started rather cautiously for the Italian national team. During the first few stages, a young man from the Paris suburbs, Jacques Marinelli, took command. Nevertheless, everyone knew that the race would be played out in the Pyrenees or the Alps.

The first demonstration of the "Campionissimo" in this Tour took place in the 57-mile time trial, between Sables-d'Olonne and La Rochelle, which Coppi won. Jacques Goddet, the Tour director, didn't lack superlatives: "Impossible to hate the movement which shifts the lines when Fausto Coppi, perched on his bike, pedals in a style that is as pure as the Divine Comedy. He then becomes the 'one and only.'"

But the Pyrenees did not create the expected upset, even if Coppi still proved himself the best during the Pau-Luchon stage. So everyone awaited the Alps.

The first great battle was set to unfold between Cannes and Briançon.

At the foot of the Izoard, Coppi and Bartali, who had teamed up in order to win, took the stage. In 12 miles of climbing, they would gain 3:30 on 1947 Tour winner Jean Robic and more than 4 minutes over the other favorites.

As they entered the rock-strewn *Casse déserte,* a fitting backdrop to the Tour, nobody cared about what was going on behind. All that mattered were the two Italians. Coppi took the Izoard in the lead, with Bartali beside him. But the Tuscan punctured and the Piedmontese waited for him!

"Impossible to hate the movement which shifts the lines when Fausto Coppi, perched on his bike, pedals in a style that is as pure as the Divine Comedy. He then becomes the 'one and only.'" (Jacques Goddet)

Tour de France 1952. The unofficial verdict had already fallen. Coppi, the supreme, lets Robic and Ockers fight it out in the Pyrenees passes. On the right, Carrea, Coppi's right-hand man, keeps an eye on the whole business. The Campionissimo is at the very back. He would soon break away to win alone in Pau.

The vertiginous descent toward Briançon began, but it was Bartali's birthday and Coppi decided to give him the victory; Bartali thus took the yellow jersey.

There still remained the second battle in the Alps, between Briançon and Saint-Vincent d'Aosta, over the Montgenèvre, Mont Cenis, Iseran and Petit-Saint-Bernard passes. At first, the stage was a struggle between Bartali and Robic but then, in the last few bends before the summit of the Col d'Iseran, Coppi came out of hiding. In just a hundred meters he took out Stan Ockers and "Apo" Lazaridès, devoured Bartali, left Robic standing and shot off on his own toward the summit. On the descent, he would be caught by a small group that included, among others, Bartali.

On the Petit-Saint-Bernard, Coppi and Bartali found themselves attacking together on their own. The two champions crossed onto Italian soil to the kind of cheers and adulation that one can only imagine. But pretty soon Bartali, at the bottom of the descent, raised his arm. He had fallen victim to a puncture. Then, betrayed by a slippery road, he fell. Coppi asked his directeur sportif what action he should take. He was instructed to continue alone. There were 26 miles left to go before Saint-Vincent d'Aosta. Coppi gobbled them up as if putting on a show, and arrived 5 minutes in front of Bartali to relieve him of the yellow jersey.

It is interesting to note that on the mountain between the foot of the Col d'Aubisque in the Pyrenees and the summit of Aosta in the Alps, Coppi took 57 minutes out of Jacques Marinelli, the best-placed Frenchman in the general classification, all the time taking care of Bartali. What mastery! Could there really be a better way to exploit the mountain roads, with their climbs, descents and valleys?

In winning this Tour de France, Coppi notched up another exploit: winning both the national tours of Italy and France the same year for the first time in history. He controlled the peloton, which was subjugated by the astounding choreography of this soloist whose aesthetic harmony reached the sublime.

In 1952, he won the Tour of Italy, but when asked to ride the Tour de France, he once more disapproved of Bartali's presence. "All that you're interested in," he cried to him, "is arriving in Paris in front of me!"

Only the diplomacy of Alfredo Binda was able to bring the two individuals to an agreement, and they both turned up at the start in Brest.

Coppi didn't hang about to assert his presence, during the fifth stage, and then in the seventh stage time trial from Metz to Nancy.

His teammates did not remain idle, controlling all the key breakaways. Fiorenzo Magni took the yellow jersey, before it passed to Coppi's most faithful domestique, Andrea "Sandrino" Carrea, in Lausanne, at the end of the ninth stage. Coppi had said to him, a little annoyed: "Ride your own race and watch who you like."

"With 86 miles to go," remembers Carrea, "10 men attacked: Marinelli, Rémy, Diggelmann and a few others. I went with them and, the more the miles passed, the more of a lead our group took. Diggelmann won on home ground, in Switzerland. I went straight to the hotel where, a few minutes later, the police turned up looking for me. It was rather bizarre. 'The police? But what have I done?' They answered: 'We've been ordered to escort you back to the finishing line, because you've won the yellow jersey.' Ah! You bet I was shocked. Me, the leader of the Tour de France, in front of Fausto? You must be joking? I was scared, really scared. I kept telling myself: 'How will Coppi take this?' And so I put on the yellow jersey. I can remember crying. I looked for Fausto and when I found him, I went straight to him; I cried even harder. 'Why are you crying Sandrino?' 'I don't know Fausto, you know, this jersey, I know that I don't deserve it. I mean a poor boy like me, yellow jersey of the Tour, do you realize that Fausto?' "

But Carrea would not keep his golden jersey for long. Just one day. The next day, Robic sparked off the battle on the Alpe-d'Huez climb, then a rough, dirt road. Coppi responded and dealt with everyone, like a berserk warrior, or a wild beast pouncing on its prey.

He won the stage and took the yellow jersey for the second time in his career. He would never give it up, crushing the whole of the peloton again the next day in the stage from Bourg-d'Oisans to Sestriere and winning by a KO after having dominated on the climbs.

A huge roar greeted his arrival in Sestriere. There was a wait of a little over 7 minutes before the second man turned up, the Spaniard Bernardo Ruiz, and more than 10 minutes before Bartali arrived.

The scenes at the finish became frenzied. The police lines were broken and Coppi was tugged at and dragged along, and eventually saved by a reserve unit of armed police.

The Tour was already over. The Italian's superiority had engendered a certain disinterest or even boredom and sadness in both journalists and riders. To no one's surprise, the Tour organizers announced that they were going to increase the amount of prize money awarded to the second-

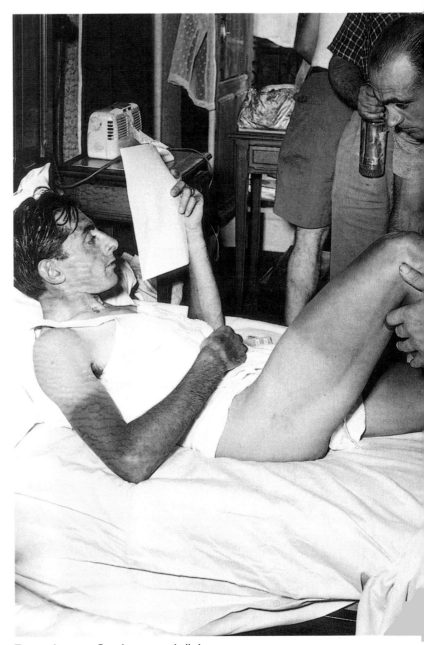

To remain great, Coppi renounced all the pleasures of life. His three watchwords were: training, competition and rest. He never wavered from them.

Tour de France 1951, Coppi and Hugo Koblet soared away from the rest. The Italian found a Swiss in a state of grace: Koblet would triumph over Coppi in Luchon and win the Tour.

Opposite: Coppi in search of the yellow jersey. He is only on a bike, and yet his limbs take on an incomparable harmony, while at the same time giving an impression of fragility and vulnerability. That is doubtless where his strange magnetism came from.

His mother, Héléna, came all the way to the Parc des Princes to see Koblet's victory in the 1951 Tour de France.

and third-place riders in the general classification by 500,000 and 250,000 francs respectively.

Nothing seemed capable of tripping up Coppi, who once more took the Tour of Italy-Tour de France double. This would nevertheless be his last appearance in the Great Tour.

The former Tour winner André Leducq would say: "I ask myself whether there has ever been a winner in the history of the Tour who has been able to combine such strength, wisdom, patience and race savvy."

Hugo Koblet; "the Pedaler of Charm"

And then came Koblet…and all that was so structured, solid and flowing in cycling at the beginning of the 1950s seemed ridiculously petty and outmoded.

He was a kind of divinity, enlightening a pack of hounds called the peloton. His beauty and his skill shone all around. His position on the bike made one want to just leap

French singer Edith Piaf visits Hugo Koblet after the first stage of the 1953 Tour, while the radio broadcasts his most recent success.

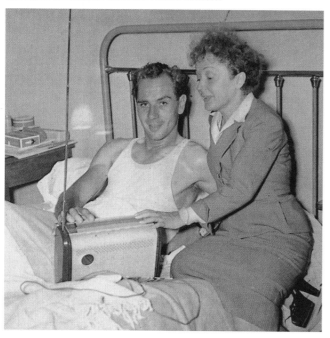

on, and the humorist Jacques Grello baptized him..."the Pedaler of Charm."

In 1950, he became the first foreigner to win the Tour of Italy, before winning the Tour of Switzerland. The impression that he left on his adversaries was one of incredulity. Thus it was that André Mahé, an excellent cyclist of the post-war period, who had just abandoned the Tour of Switzerland and was on his way home, stopped off in Annecy to greet the riders in the *Dauphiné Libéré* race. He came across Maurice Vidal, the editor-in-chief of *Miroir Sprint,* astonished, one can well imagine, to find him there.

"I abandoned the Tour of Switzerland," he told the journalist. "I thought that I had proven that I was a cyclist. Now I wonder what I'm doing in this business."

"Heck, what happened to you?"

"What happened was that there I was, sweating blood and tears to climb the passes, when I suddenly see a guy climbing up next to me without a drop of sweat. It got me down to see him climb such a difficult slope, holding the handlebars with one hand and sometimes letting go completely to comb his hair. I'm quite prepared to suffer on a bike but I don't like being humiliated."

There was Koblet at the start of the 1951 Tour de France, in Metz. The papers were declaring Louison Bobet as the favorite, in front of him. The Swiss had clearly predicted beforehand that Koblet would win the seventh stage, a time-trial, from La Guerche to Angers, and win it he did.

Even though the prediction proved correct, the stage nearly finished badly. The judges actually announced Bobet the winner. Koblet frowned and asked to see the times. The correct result pronounced Koblet as the winner. The judge Raoul Adam had in fact given Koblet an extra minute in error. It was incredible, in the view of reporter Georges Briquet: "To be called Adam and be incapable of naming the first man!"

Koblet had not as yet taken the yellow jersey but he could already see the light.

Everything suddenly exploded during the eleventh stage from Brive to Agen. At mile 29, Koblet found himself on his own. There were 80 miles to go and the riders were crossing the Corrèze, the Lot and the edge of the Gramat plateau. The Swiss up front clearly did not know the meaning of the words "prudence" and "economy." His torso inclined over the handlebars, his admirably slender legs leaning slightly together at knee-level, he did not give the impression of going all out. At one point, in a section buffeted by the wind, he lost a minute on his pursuers, but his re-acceleration was phenomenal and on the plain between Souillac and Pont Carral, his lead widened to nearly 4 minutes. The peloton behind him was left stunned and subdued.

Ever clearheaded, he crossed the finish line and found the audacity, before the astounded spectators, to consult his excellent Swiss stopwatch. Result: 2:35 lead. And he still didn't have the yellow jersey, even though he was ahead of all the great favorites: Raphël Géminiani, Lucien Lazaridès, Bobet and Coppi, incredulous men who unanimously affirmed "We did all we could to catch him."

"If he climbs like he races on the flat," declared Géminiani, "then we can say good-bye to the yellow jersey. None of us will wear it. If he doesn't have any problems, then we can all start looking for another job."

The prediction was confirmed in the Pyrenees, with Coppi and Koblet dominating their rivals. Koblet beat Coppi in Luchon and took the yellow jersey.

From then on he paraded his golden mantle with style, dominating in Montpellier and on Mont Ventoux. He let Coppi take the tough Izoard stage before winning again, on home ground, in Geneva, thronged with a sea of supporters.

The Parc des Princes was yet another triumph for Koblet and the end of a wonderful story. In 1964, an awful fate awaited him, though. He, the prodigal child emanating kindness and style, was not clever with handling money. He completely failed to come to grips with this bright new world and his life ended in a traffic accident. Did he kill himself because of a marital problem? Was it perhaps really just an accident? The great mystery remains.

He was so handsome, the fine Hugo. He had it all—elegance personified, elegance in movement, and elegance by nature.

The wonderful legend
of Louison Bobet

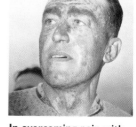

In overcoming pain with dignity, Bobet built one of the best-ever lists of career wins.

For the love of Christiane, Louison Bobet won three consecutive Tours de France for the first time ever in the history of the Tour.

Opposite: Louison Bobet, longtime holder of the yellow jersey in the 1948 Tour, had to give way to Bartali's dazzling offensives. Behind him, radio reporter Jacques Sallebert prepares to step in.

In towns and villages, all await the Tour, ready to point out the yellow jersey. Here, crowds in Faou, Finistère pay tribute to a local son (by marriage), Lucien Teisseire (Tour de France 1954).

When Gino Bartali won the Tour de France in 1948, he didn't hide the fact that he considered Louison Bobet to be a future winner of the race. That year, Bobet had earned his first-ever yellow jersey, at the end of the third stage from Dinard to Nantes, taking it from the Belgian Jan Engels. He lost his trophy the next day to the Belgian Lambrecht, before taking it back again in Biarritz, at the foot of the Pyrenees.

The sordid atmosphere in the French team, managed by Maurice Archambaud, had not escaped the attention of the press, including Jean Leulliot who wrote in *Miroir Sprint:* "The French team is composed of a bunch of stars, all of them as selfish as the next…. They have never supported or assisted Bobet as they should have done."

If Bobet's morale was already hit by this state of affairs, then he could have done without the attack of boils which broke out all over his body. His left foot became deformed. But he was so driven, that he pushed himself to win the stage at Cannes after having climbed the Col de Turini, enduring real agony. Worse was to come though. The next day, on the Col d'Allos, his bike fell apart under him. He was given a spare machine, but it was Robic's and so the frame was too small. This was due to a major error of Archambaud, who had assumed that Robic was the only potential victor in the team. When Bobet finally found a bike that fitted his size, it was too late. Bartali was prancing in front and Louison lost his jersey the following day, in Aix-les-Bains. But what courage!

Although he had many worthy finishes, he would have to wait until 1953 before finding the golden fleece that took him to victory in the Tour de France.

It has been written that Bobet's greatest achievements were always born from the greatest pain. In this Tour of 1953, he was again suffering from boils when the Pyrenees arrived. His personal doctor, Dr. Maros, rushed straight from Brittany, whipped out his scalpel and lanced the boils, before giving the cyclist a radiotherapy session.

Robic showed himself to be the great man of the Pyrenees, although he didn't gain much time over the other favorites at the finish in Luchon, after crossing the great passes. The law of the strongest would soon impose itself in the Alps.

But the idea of a bellicose Robic was enough to irritate the French team into deciding to pull out all the stops even before they had reached the Alps on the stage from Albi to Béziers. Bobet and three teammates led a nine-man break that splintered the field. Robic was beaten, even his Brittany teammate Malléjac became the race leader. Now the storm started to rumble in the heart of the French team. Nello Lauredi had won the stage, thus depriving Bobet of the first-place time bonus. That evening, at dinner, the debate was fierce. The situation did have the merit of clarifying positions, with Bobet being affirmed as the sole leader of the French team.

Malléjac was still in the yellow jersey starting the eighteenth stage from Gap to Briançon. Adolphe Deledda, a loyal domestique on the French team, went on the attack, accompanied by regional team riders Bernard Quennehen and Jean Dacquay. Deledda led at the summit of the Vars and then, warned by a motorcyclist that Bobet had just broken away with the Spaniard Jesus Lorono, he readied himself to take his team leader through the Guil valley and the Queyras gorges up to the foot of the Izoard.

Bobet descended the Vars at breakneck speed. Very skillfully, adroit on his bike, with a steady eye and iron will, it was very clear where his intentions lay. At the foot of the pass, Deledda was waiting for him. He was on his own now, just like Bobet who had left Lorono behind. Deledda rode like a maniac, pouring all of his energy toward the common victory. When he slowed up, completely exhausted, he left Bobet to his destiny. The backdrop of the Izoard slid past him. He attacked the "giant" with a strange serenity, conscious of his worth and his superiority. Nothing could stop him now; both the yellow jersey and the Tour itself lay at his feet. It was a great moment.

With the Tour now won, Bobet fixed the following year's Tour as his next objective and decided in the meantime to add a few more trophies to his collection.

This champion with such panache would clearly continue in style.

In 1954, he was certainly considered the favorite, but he was not the only one. The Swiss riders Koblet and Ferdi Kübler were also clearly in the running. Bobet took an early lead, beating both of them in the sprint at the finish of the second stage from Antwerp to Lille. Two days later, in Rouen, he took the yellow jersey after a short team time trial.

The start of the sixth stage, from Saint-Brieuc to Brest, encouraged that thought, since Bobet was without the yellow jersey. No, he didn't lose it in the race; his sister Madeleine had left town with the jersey, which he had given to her as a present the previous day. He had simply forgotten that a new leader's jersey was no longer given every day, but every two days. So, when he went to put on his jersey, he realized his mistake too late, since the supply truck had already left for the next finish. Luckily, his soigneur, Raymond Le Bert, was from Saint-Brieuc, and Louison was able to retrieve a yellow jersey that he'd given him as a present the year before. Unfortunately the item had shrunk in the wash. Le Bert was never short on ideas though, and got a heavyweight boxer from the local gym to put it on. Some of the stitching split, but Bobet was able to wear his old yellow jersey. He would give it up legitimately to the Dutchman Wagtmans at the end of the eighth stage from Vannes to Angers.

In the Pyrenees, Bobet replied to all of Kübler's attacks, blow for blow. The Spaniard Federico Bahamontes showed himself to be the king of the climbers, but the very clearheaded Bobet kept pace with him on the uphills, accompanied by French regional riders Gilbert Bauvin and Malléjac.

But Bobet didn't want to reclaim the yellow jersey too soon. He left it to the little Bauvin to handle this task, and didn't take the lead until Millau, when the Tour was just about to leave the Cévennes.

From then on, it was hard to see who could possibly break the balance and unity of this superb French team.

Tour de France 1953. A long discussion took place between the members of the French team. In the end they decided that Bobet seemed the strongest to take the yellow jersey and win the Tour. Louison and his right-hand man, Géminiani, make their plans.

A vigilant Louison Bobet in the yellow jersey during the 1954 Tour (fifteenth stage). His teammate Jean Forestier helps him while Gilbert Bauvin, on the right, has to content himself with his regional status again, after having lost the overall lead to Bobet the previous day in Millau.

Bobet once more soared off on the Izoard and so won his second Tour de France a quarter-hour ahead of Kübler.

The third would be more difficult to pull off. As in 1954, he wanted to assure himself of a psychological advantage from the start, and duly won the third stage at the citadel of Namur. Antonin Rolland soon picked up the yellow jersey for the French team, which would later have to reckon with the arrival of the Luxembourg rider Charly Gaul, the infinitely sublime "Angel of the Mountains," particularly in the Alps and the Pyrenees. Bobet won the Ventoux stage in magnificent style, but he was suffering. His saddle sores had reappeared and, alone in his room, he would sometimes cry out in pain. But this was no moment to give in. He instructed his men: "Don't leave the way open for the Luxembourg guy."

Six days later, on the Toulouse-Saint-Gaudens stage, Gaul and Bobet climbed the passes together. Gaul won the stage by a minute, with Bobet taking the yellow jersey. But then a new danger arrived, Jean Brankart, a Walloon who won the Pau stage. The Belgian would be a threat on the 43-mile time trial from Châtellerault to Tours. Could he beat Bobet? He managed to take the stage, but the challenge came too late and Bobet became the first in history to win the Tour de France three times in a row.

"I seized it rather than won it," the French champion admitted. "That is why out of all three, this was the one with the most prizes, the prizes of courage and will."

Louison Bobet had pushed his physical resistance almost to its limit and his saddle sore had become an open wound. At the beginning of November 1955 he had to undergo an operation. It was definitely time; if the injury had been ignored a few months longer, his life would have been in danger.

Jacques Anquetil, the man for every challenge

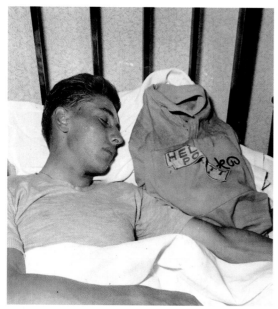

The yellow jersey dreams (Tour de France 1957).

Opposite: Tour de France 1961. Anquetil bet that he would take the yellow jersey the first day and keep it until the end. He won his bet. Charly Gaul, third in the Tour, is next to him.

Anquetil's grasp was firm even before the mountains. Here he is winning the stage in Thonon-les-Bains (Tour de France 1957).

T he storm rumbled over the Hainaut. The 1957 Tour de France entered the fifth stage's final phase between Roubaix and Charleroi.

Jean Bobet, Fernand Picot, Daan De Groot and two members of the French team, Gilbert Bauvin and Jacques Anquetil headed the race. Anquetil was seeking the first yellow jersey of his career. The rain came on stronger, as did the ardor of this young Norman riding his first Tour at age twenty-three. Oh, how Jacques hurt the others, with his long stints! When he learned that a group of twelve counterattackers was approaching, he bent a little more over his bike, his nose nearly touching the stem, like the born track rider he was. The pace increased a little and Picot had to sprint to keep up. De Groot showed signs of weakening.

The gap grew wider and victory was saved. Bauvin won the stage and Anquetil found himself wearing yellow, five days after starting the Tour for the first time. This was an exploit worthy of an exceptional champion.

"We feared he would suffer from the hard labor of the Tour," wrote Jacques Goddet in l'Equipe. "And he has just taken these first five terrible days without batting an eyelid. The stars of stage-racing collapsed, foundered, barely hung. He was serene, with a glowing face that was almost completely relaxed. He covered all the shifts in the race and showed himself the master of his skills that he used perfectly. A pleasant comrade and a good teammember, it was all a total success for him."

Anquetil found himself deftly slipped into the Tour at the last moment. Louison Bobet and Raphaël Géminiani wanted to remain the sole rulers of the Grande Boucle, and didn't want to contend with Anquetil. But Bobet, worn down by the war of nerves in the Tour of Italy, where he had to defend the pink jersey with all his strength against an Italian tidal wave, declared, on the shores of the Adriatic: "I am not ready, mentally, to take part in the Tour de France. I am

In 1957, at the Parc des Princes, Bobet and Anquetil fight over the yellow jersey. In truth, a transfer of power was taking place.

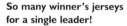

So many winner's jerseys for a single leader!

thirty-two years old; it's the younger generation's turn—a back-handed allusion to Anquetil. The young man was offered great responsibilities and did not turn them down, supported by his friend André Darrigade.

Anquetil started by winning in his hometown of Rouen, at the end of the third day, then took over the yellow jersey at Charleroi. Although he lost the emblem during the stage from Metz to Colmar, the French team's Jean Forestier won it back the next day.

During the tenth stage from Thonon-les-Bains to Briançon, the Galibier climb enabled Anquetil to confirm his potential. In this stage, he was held up by numerous technical problems all the way through the Maurienne valley, but he didn't worry too much about the advance being carried out by the leading trio of Gastone Nencini, Marcel Janssens and Bauvin—his faithful teammate. Anquetil's excellent morale even led him to snatch a flask of chilled champagne from the president of the Sallanches Cycle Club. Although this flask cost Forestier the yellow jersey, it perked up his team-leader. But Marcel Bidot, their directeur sportif, was rather concerned that Anquetil was 5 minutes behind the leading group. Something had to be done.

Anquetil obeyed. The champagne had given him a slight lift and he now felt a strong urge to pick up the pace. Over the last 2½ miles of the Galibier he took 2 minutes out of Janssens and Nencini, now on their own. At the finish, where the Italian won, Anquetil had conceded only 1:18 and so took back the yellow jersey. He would never let it go again, despite a momentary weak spot in the Pyrenees. Even then, he showed an amazing capacity for recuperation. He won the twentieth-stage time trial on a rather acrobatic 41-mile course at Bordeaux in an average speed of more than 26 miles per hour. The journalist Roger Bastide wrote: "Already, Napoleon is becoming Bonaparte."

Anquetil didn't return victorious to the Tour de France until 1961, having won the 1960 Tour of Italy in the meantime. Exasperated by the critics who reproached him for having won just a single Tour de France, he declared that he would take the yellow jersey the first day and keep it till the end. He kept his word. Gaul finished second. Over twenty-one stages, the Frenchman transformed competitive cycling into an exact science.

In 1962, doubts set in though. Beaten in the Tour of Spain by his teammate Rudi Altig, Anquetil nonetheless declared unambiguously: "On the road, I want to be the boss."

Altig won two stages in the first three days, wearing

Champions all! From left to right: Rudi Altig (World Pursuit Champion), Raymond Poulidor (French Road Champion), Rik Van Looy (World Road Champion) and Jacques Anquetil (Tour Winner), at the start of the Criterium des As 1961.

Roger Rivière and Anquetil had something in common. Both of them had beaten the world hour record. All that the man from Saint-Etienne was missing was the Tour yellow jersey. He set off to get it in 1960 when his cycling career took a tumble during the descent of the Col du Perjuret (stage from Millau to Avignon).

the yellow jersey in the same Tour in which Raymond Poulidor was making his debut. Four days before the start Poulidor fractured the little finger on his left hand, and so did not play a leading role in the Tour.

Anquetil struck out hard in the eighth-stage time trial between Luçon and La Rochelle: 29½ mph average speed.

So there he was on his way. Little by little he crept up on the yellow jersey, which never stopped changing hands. In the Pyrenees, on the ascent of Superbagnères—an 11½-mile time trial—he was beaten by the born climber Bahamontes. The yellow jersey now went to the Belgian Joseph Planckaert who doggedly defended it, particularly on the stage from Briançon to Aix-les-Bains through the cols of the Chartreuse, where he stuck to Jacques Anquetil like a leech.

"What should I do?" he asked his team director, Raphaël Géminiani. "Even on the descents, when I'm riding flat out, I can feel him behind me. I know that if I fall, he'll fall on top of me, if I crack he'll shoot off and if I dawdle along, then he'll do exactly the same."

But there still remained the fine time trial and Anquetil won it majestically, on the 42 miles between Bourgoin and Lyon, over narrow, rolling roads, beating Planckaert by nearly 5 minutes. So Anquetil won his second Tour, although it would not be his most memorable, since he would have preferred to have won it in the mountains and not in the time trials. The public was not satisfied, confirmed by the whistles that greeted him at the finishing line. The lesson was learned. Henceforth, in order to silence his critics, he wanted to prove himself the master of the mountains in the 1963 Tour. An awesome challenge. The course hardly put him at an advantage, though, as the stage finishes in the high mountains were located very close to the last pass. The climbers Bahamontes and Poulidor rubbed their hands with glee.

From left to right: Vittorio Adorni, Poulidor, Anquetil and Van Looy.

Anquetil was the first to win five Tours de France. Here he rides next to the Spanish climber Federico Bahamontes, whom he managed to fend off even in the mountains.

Anquetil had to fight off Bahamontes throughout his career. After the Spaniard's victorious Tour (1959), the 1960s witnessed the glorious breakaways of the "Eagle of Toledo," who managed to contain the strong Frenchman.

The metamorphosis did happen. Over the Aubisque and Tourmalet passes, glued to his handlebars, crouched over his bike, concentrated and pugnacious, Anquetil wiped out all the attacks. But he did not yet take the yellow jersey, which was held by the Belgian Gilbert Desmet.

After the Pyrenees, everyone was talking about Anquetil, who had made a huge impression on the peloton. Nevertheless, the great favorite was still Bahamontes. The Spaniard won the stage in Grenoble and took the yellow jersey in Val-d-Isère, the Frenchman only 3 seconds behind. Bahamontes had to put some distance between himself and his rival in the stage from Grenoble to Val-d'Isère. And the route seemed designed for him. So?

So, Anquetil, urged on by directeur sportif Géminiani, refused to be beaten. For several evenings, the two men had been studying the Col de la Forclaz in great detail. The clever Géminiani, came up with a plan to get around the rules. Anquetil would use a light bike, fitted with a 46 x 20 gear, but since the descent was potholed, he would need another, heavier bike. Changing one's bike was forbidden, however. Géminiani thus readied himself to pull a rabbit out of his hat.

Poulidor began the hostilities by tearing into the Forclaz at the start of the ascent, but he soon ran of steam. Bahamontes, who had left the peloton, passed him at full acceleration with Anquetil in his wake. Anquetil was in total control. Bahamontes couldn't shake him off. The man from Toledo tried everything, constantly changing pace, standing up on the pedals, sitting down again…but there was nothing to be done. Anquetil, astride his light bike, easily matched his pace.

At the summit, Géminiani prepared to intervene to change Anquetil's bike, but how could he do this when a race commissaire had taken a seat in his car, and was responsible for monitoring the proper running of the race?

Connivance worked wonders.

Approaching the banner, the Norman quickly looked at Géminiani and, a moment later, stopped and shouted: "My derailleur!"

"Merde!" cried out Géminiani in turn, addressing the inspector. "He's broken his derailleur."

The bike was perfectly all right, but the mechanic, warned in advance, immediately leapt out of the car with a pair of pliers and swiftly cut the derailleur's cable. The inspector, having seen nothing, could only note that the cable was indeed "broken." Meanwhile, Anquetil had set off again on another bike, kept ready for precisely such a mechanical problem. He caught up with Bahamontes on the descent, beat him in the sprint at Chamonix and took the yellow jersey. He thus won the Tour de France before even completing the final time trial.

He had become the first person to attain four Tour de France wins.

In 1964, Anquetil and Poulidor fought a long and drawn-out duel. The Limousin, who was enjoying un-equalled popularity, had a clear sight of Tour victory. He was certainly capable of it. Anquetil had been warned.

Poulidor showed his strength in the seventh stage from Champagnole to Thonon-les-Bains by way of the Col de la Faucille, managing to join a breakaway group of 15 riders. Anquetil, inattentive, lost 34 seconds to his rival. The blow to his morale became physical the next day, when approaching Briançon. Near the summit of the Galibier, Anquetil dropped back, his legs worn out and his heart beating wildly. Riding on courage, he chased hard in the descent, but still conceded 47 seconds to Poulidor. It was a bad day.

The next day, with his batteries miraculously recharged, Anquetil rode strongly up the Restefond and won the stage in Monaco. He then executed a heavenly time trial from Hyères to Toulon, which left him only 1:11 behind the yellow jersey worn by the young Georges Groussard.

Since leaving Rennes, Anquetil seemed haunted by the prediction of a psychic named Belline who had plainly declared: "Anquetil will drop out of the Tour near Andorra."

The riders arrived there, and took a rest day. Anquetil eagerly accepted an invitation to partake in a huge roast sheep barbecue that had been organized for the race followers. He not only did honor to the roast, but also drank to his heart's content.

The next day, when the peloton attacked the Col d'Envalira, the Norman champion immediately started to lose ground. He had never liked fast starts. Were the psychic Belline's predictions coming true? Anquetil was fighting through a very thick fog, that was for sure. He reached the summit with great difficulty, aided by his teammate Louis Rostollan. Géminiani passed him a flask of champagne. He felt better after that and zoomed off, riding straight by his teammates who were waiting for him, drawn on by this sixth sense that cyclists sometimes have: double sight. He never slowed up, nor braked. At the bottom of the descent, he finally caught up with his rivals Jan Janssen, Henri Anglade and the yellow jersey Groussard. But the really unlucky one that day would be Poulidor, who fell while changing bikes and conceded almost 3 minutes by the finish in Toulouse. Not being one to give up easily, Poulidor promptly won the next day in Luchon, and climbed to within 9 seconds of Anquetil who calmly widened the gap again to 56

Anquetil wearing the yellow jersey, revered as the finest and most refined pedaling machine in the world. The public followed him with admiration, yet general opinion would have wished him to have been a little less perfect and to have seen some chinks in his armor. They preferred Poulidor whose repeated defeats in the Tour made him seem closer to their own mortality.

THE LEGEND OF THE PUY-DE-DÔME

One of the most wonderful skirmishes in the Tour de France (1964). Anquetil (yellow jersey) and Poulidor start the ascent of the Puy-de-Dôme. One of them was attempting to bluff the other. But which one? Poulidor would eventually forge ahead of his rival 1500 meters from the line. Anquetil surpassed himself to stem the hemorrhage of seconds…and finally managed it. The yellow jersey was saved by just 14 seconds.

seconds at the end of the seventeenth-stage time trial at Bayonne, where he dispossessed Groussard of the yellow jersey.

There now began one of the most famous duels in the history of cycling.

It was July 12, 1964. The front group of 30 riders was about to tackle the ultra-steep climb up the Puy-de-Dôme. Jerseys soaked with sweat, their faces dripping and staring steadily ahead, there was both hope and fear in this squad of racers, where the yellow jersey of Anquetil and the deep purple tunic of Poulidor were already climbing side by side. Spanish climber Julio Jimenez broke away, and after him went Bahamontes, but the main focus of attention was elsewhere.

Shoulder to shoulder, Anquetil and Poulidor continued to climb the slope. They kept the same pace; Poulidor might have been two centimeters ahead. Who was bluffing whom? If only one or the other of them knew. "I was bad that day and Raymond was good," declared Anquetil later, with Poulidor adding the sweet euphemism: "Neither of us was excellent."

There were 1500 meters left to the banner. How would this unbearable suspense end? Suddenly, Anquetil started to slip back, centimeter by centimeter, to 2 meters. He tried to find the most effective position on his bike, his face drained of blood. Poulidor was breaking away. Anquetil was nearly dying on his bike.

At the white line, the stopwatches automatically clicked and registered that the Limousin Anquetil had taken 42 seconds off the Norman. Just 14 seconds kept the yellow jersey safe. He jow felt the Tour was won, since only a final 17-mile time trial remained. Poulidor still had a chance, but wasn't Jacques the master of this specialty? Poulidor initially held his own, but Anquetil went on to beat him by 21 seconds, and take the Tour by a measly 55 seconds. A record fifth victory for Anquetil.

He was without doubt one of the most marvelous pedaling machines in the world, reminding us of what Jean Cocteau said of Radiguet in his preface to *Count Orgel's Ball:* "He was one of those rare beings for whom life is too short."

Bernard Thévenet unseats the idol

Ever since he took second place in the 1973 Tour de France behind Luis Ocaña, following his stage wins on Mont Ventoux and the Ballon d'Alsace after receiving serious injuries in 1972, Bernard Thévenet became one of the most likely candidates for a Tour victory. Magnificent winner of the Dauphiné Libéré in 1975, he was one of the pre-race fa-

Bernard Thévenet will always be remembered as the one who knocked Eddy Merckx of his hitherto untouchable pedestal. A stylish cyclist, and fanatic of "a job well done," he always sought to make a race that was full of twists and turns as spectacular as possible. Here, he pulls out all the stops in his pursuit of the yellow jersey and his second Tour victory (1977).

vorites at the Tour. The man from Burgundy, in brilliant form, did not appear surprised by this. Only the opinion of Jacques Anquetil annoyed him a little. The Norman stated in *Cyclisme Magazine* that Thévenet could become a brilliant second-place man…like Poulidor.

Second to Merckx, of course. But didn't the first time trial prove Anquetil right? Merckx won it at an average speed of more than 30½ mph on the 10-mile Saint-Jean-de-Monts course; Thévenet only managed sixth place, almost a minute back. But this was just the beginning. He did better, a lot better, a few days later in Auch. In this hilly 33½-mile time trial he finished only 9 seconds behind the world champion, who confessed: "I know now where the danger is going to come from. He's called Thévenet and his performance in the time trial was all too clear!"

Merckx buckled in the Pyrenees, but didn't break. Thévenet nibbled away at his lead bit by bit and, by the fourteenth-stage finish on the Puy-de-Dôme—where Merckx was punched in the kidneys by a stupid spectator—the Charolais came within 58 seconds of the yellow jersey worn by King Eddy. The decisive moments would come in the Alps.

On the stage from Nice to Pra-Loup, guided by his Peugeot team director Maurice de Muer, Thévenet planned to attack up the Col du Champs, a first-category climb, which was making its debut appearance in the Tour de France.

The plan was put into action, with Thévenet attacking once, twice and so on all the way up. Each time Merckx, perfectly composed, responded. At the summit, the yellow jersey even mounted a strong counterattack, so as to keep his psychological advantage. During the descent, Thévenet thought that all was lost. Fortunately, his teammate Raymond Delisle arrived just at the right moment to lift his spirits. The Burgundian mustered his courage and morale, buoyed by his Norman comrade. The two of them caught up with the Merckx group at the foot of the Col d'Allos. Its summit was only 14 miles from the finish, but those miles included the big climb up to Pra-Loup.

On the Allos, Merckx once more went onto the offensive. Thévenet hung on, even though the Belgian had gone into overdrive. The summit approached, just 800 meters or so away. Just got to hang on…. Merckx didn't weaken and it was Thévenet who had to let go. Under the banner on the Col d'Allos, Thévenet was 15 seconds back.

That gap soon widened as the yellow jersey swept down the descent, with the race followers assuming that he was soaring toward another victory. Thévenet sensed that everything was collapsing.

Onwards, ever onwards toward the consecration. (Tour de France 1975).

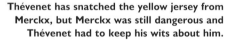

Thévenet has snatched the yellow jersey from Merckx, but Merckx was still dangerous and Thévenet had to keep his wits about him.

Thévenet will shortly take his second Tour de France. Van Impe (right) and Zoetemelk (far left) were his toughest adversaries right up until the end.

Soon only the last ascent remained: the climb toward Pra-Loup. Merckx tackled it strongly, but suddenly showed signs of fatigue. His energy was gone. He struggled, barely moving. The Italian ace Felice Gimondi passed him, astonished, unused to such a sight. Behind them, Thévenet continued to work his way up the field, catching Lucien Van Impe and Joop Zoetemelk. He finally caught sight of Merckx on a little straight stretch. Bit by bit, the situation reversed itself. The Burgundian was finally feeling stronger and it was now Thévenet's turn to play the locomotive. He stood up on his pedals and, inspired, forgot his companions and went straight for the Belgian. He hesitated a moment, unsure of how to take him, then gathered all his remaining strength and dealt the coup de grâce.

"I passed Merckx without even daring to look at him," recalls Thévenet. "I knew he was spent and I could understand what he was suffering, but when you find yourself in such a state of grace, you're pedaling in another world. That's what happened to me. I caught up with Gimondi in the same way a mile from the finish. I heard the crowd screaming my name, and I thought of the yellow jersey, without really believing it, and of my Peugeot teammates, and I told myself that, at dinner, we would have to forget our athlete's diet, for the champagne would be flowing…."

The stopwatch showed the following: Thévenet beat Gimondi by 23 seconds and Merckx, who was in fifth place and had been passed by Zoetemelk and Van Impe, by 1:56. And so in this ski-station in the Alpes-de-Haute-Provence, Bernard Thévenet put on the first yellow jersey of his career. The Tour was virtually won, even though he still had to ensure that his guard didn't drop, and he would have to watch out for any possible attacks from Merckx in the second alpine stage from Barcelonnette to Serre-Chevalier.

But Thévenet asserted himself by shooting off on the Izoard. And at the finish in Serre-Chevalier, Merckx confessed: "I lost the Tour today!"

After a catastrophic season in 1976, would Thévenet be able to pull himself out of the abyss in 1977? The subject was earnestly debated in the press. Thévenet announced that the Tour was his prime objective.

He had just lost the Dauphiné Libéré by only 9 seconds, ceding victory to the rising French star Bernard Hinault who, still too young, would delay his start in the Grande Boucle for a while longer. Thévenet strongly believed in his chances, while the press refused to make him their outright Tour favorite.

The first part of the race was hardly convincing, with the sprinters engaged in a cat fight. For starters, the prologue

Tour de France 1975; sixteenth stage. Thévenet rides majestically against a stately backdrop that is right in his class, the Col de l'Izoard.

smiled favorably on the German Dietrich Thurau who beat Gerrie Knetemann and Merckx. The next day, in Auch, Pierre-Raymond Villemiane took the first stage. Thurau successfully defended his yellow jersey, by beating the very same Villemiane in a sprint finish to the Pyrenees stage from Auch to Pau over the Aspin, Tourmalet and Aubisque passes. Fourteen men broke away and carved out a big lead for themselves in this tricky stage. Thurau continued to wear the yellow jersey, but the papers complained of the riders' lack of competitiveness and spoke of an "excruciating" show. It was clear that from now on the Tour de France would go to one of the protagonists: Thurau, Merckx, Thévenet, Hennie Kuiper, Raymond Delisle.

So while the Alps approached, it was still the German Thurau who paraded his youthful physique at the head of the race. Only two minutes separated the first eight riders in the general classification, and the real battle would start on the 8.7-mile uphill time trial from Morzine to Avoriaz. Zoetemelk beat Van Impe and Thévenet—who became the yellow jersey. Thurau, the new golden-boy of the Tour, had lost the lead, but not his morale. The next day, the man who everyone called "Didi" took the sixteenth stage, from Avoriaz to Chamonix by way of the Col de la Forclaz, while a fading Eddy Merckx was struck down by dysentery. Thévenet kept his leader's jersey, although he was startled by Kuiper who won the stage the next day at Alpe-d'Huez, taking 41 seconds off Thévenet. The yellow jersey was hanging on by just 8 seconds!

To clinch success, there remained the 31-mile time trial in Dijon. The duel was going to be fierce, with no quarter given. The Tour de France was at stake.

After his first lap of the circuit, the yellow jersey had a lead of 32 seconds. Kuiper fought back to concede a final deficit of 28 seconds, and finished the Tour 48 seconds behind the Frenchman. Thévenet had run his race with intelligence and energy from the very first day.

Thévenet climbed the passes with ease. During his successful hunt for victory in the 1975 Tour he sowed much doubt in the mind of the yellow jersey, Eddy Merckx, as soon as they reached the Pyrenees passes. From then on the Belgian champion started to realize the complexity of his task.

"The Badger," one who believed

Bernard Hinault wearing the winner's yellow jersey the final day, on the Champs-Elysées. He won the Grande Boucle five times (1978, 1979, 1981, 1982 and 1985).

Opposite: At the start of his first Tour de France (1978), Hinault wore the French Champion's jersey, won just a few days before in Sarrebourg. He would soon change it to the yellow one and win his first Tour.

Tour de France 1981. Hinault was seeking to add a Tour victory to his World Championship title, after prematurely withdrawing from the Tour the previous year with a knee problem. He had lost none of his powers and dominated on every terrain.

Bernard Hinault, a one-of-a-kind real character, knew he was different from everyone else, a trait that dominated his personality. Gripped by various complexes that he found difficult to handle, he also had trouble talking about them.

His professional debut was marked by a degree of friction with Jean Stablinski, his first directeur sportif; but things got better when Cyrille Guimard took over. From Brittany, like Hinault, Guimard taught him to train in a methodical way, to establish a basic program that he would always stick to and to aim for a specific objective. He also learned to temper his violent impulses, which sometimes led him to commit serious errors. At the same time, thanks to Hinault, Guimard took great pleasure in seeing his theories proved correct.

At the start of the 1978 season, all eyes in the cycling world were fixed on Hinault. As preparation for his first Tour, he took part in the Vuelta and added the Tour of Spain to his growing list of achievements. Then, a few days before the Grande Boucle, he won the French championship at Sarrebourg. He was finally ready to excite the fans at the Tour, from start to finish.

Hinault first asserted his authority in the time trial at Sainte-Foy-la-Grande, defeating race leader Joseph Bruyère by 34 seconds, followed by Freddy Maertens, Zoetemelk and Michel Pollentier. In the Pyrenees, he matched the best climbers even when they went all-out. Hinault also showed his leadership off the bike when he led a protest by the riders at the finish of the stage in Valence-d'Agen. They were protesting the unfair system of long transfers, which cut into their rest and recuperation time. The riders, with Hinault in the lead, crossed the finish line on foot, causing the organizers to cancel the stage.

The focus now was on the 33-mile mountain time trial from Super besse to Puy-de-Dôme. Hinault faltered, losing 2 minutes to Zoetemelk and a minute to Pollentier—who now seemed in a position to win the Tour. At Alpe-d'Huez, Pollentier mounted a solo attack, forcing Bruyère to concede

Hinault knew how to ride to his limit and could recuperate extraordinarily quickly. He possessed all of the qualities that made him one of the best all-round athletes ever seen on a bike. Time trialist, climber, sprinter...was there anything that he couldn't do? Here, during the 1979 Tour, he dominates (from left to right) Raymond Martin, Johan Van der Velde, Zoop Zoetemelk and Giovanni Battaglia.

Hinault had a sense of panache and left no stone unturned. He smashed all of his rivals' strategies and became master of the peloton by his sheer power.

Decidedly insatiable, Hinault finished the 1982 Tour as he started it: with a victory the first and last day. Could he be considered anything other than an absolute conqueror?

the yellow jersey, and winning the stage by 37 seconds over Kuiper, with Hinault at 45 seconds and Zoetemelk at 1:18. Pollentier was awarded the maillot jaune, but two hours later, after cheating at the medical control, the Belgian was disqualified from the Tour. Zoetemelk became the new leader, but Hinault literally overwhelmed him in the 45-mile time trial between Metz and Nancy, taking more than 4 minutes off him. The Breton thus won the very first Tour de France he had contested, in the most elegant way.

It was the start of a long series of successes.

In 1979, while continuing to notch up other important victories, he reduced the Tour to a duel between himself and Zoetemelk that acquired a certain majesty when the two men arrived alone together on the Champs Elysées. Hinault triumphed, in a Tour where he had worn the yellow jersey for sixteen days.

After his bad luck of 1980, when he had to withdraw with an injured knee at Pau, in the middle of the Tour de France with the yellow jersey on his back. He later got his revenge by becoming the world champion at Sallanches.

Hinault returned, even stronger than before, in 1981 and 1982, when he pulled off his first Tour of Italy-Tour de France double. Then, after missing the 1983 Tour, he had an operation on his right knee. How well would he recuperate? A long period of doubt set in, and a certain Laurent Fignon was more than active during his absence.

But "the Badger" was preparing his revenge. In 1985, he returned to a Tour that was one of a kind, winning it again after having fully shown his mettle right from the prologue in Plumelec. And he carried off the Tour of Italy-Tour de France double for the second time.

Hinault was a great champion, reminding one of

Merckx by his sense for panache, and his desire to leave no stone unturned. Even though he might criticize a race, Paris-Roubaix for example, for having rather a perilous course, he still pushed himself to win it so as not to be accused of sour grapes. He was obstinate and stubborn, but had such charisma that at the end of the day people found him quite engaging.

Laurent Fignon, from dream to reality

In 1983, Bernard Hinault had been obliged to turn down the Tour de France, since he was suffering from tendinitis; the way was now clear for the ambitions of others.

Cyrille Guimard, directeur sportif of Hinault's team Renault-Gitane, undertook to pick a Tour team from his young and ambitious cyclists; its lynchpin was the duo of Laurent Fignon and Marc Madiot. Everyone knew that this was going to be a difficult Tour, due to the first week's disjointed itinerary and its many mountain stages.

Just before entering the Pyrenees, the first mountain range tackled by the Tour, Sean Kelly took the yellow jersey in Pau. Until then, he had been gobbling up bonus seconds in the various sprints, which were offered in the flat countryside to spice up the action. It would be the only yellow jersey of the Irishman's career, since the next day he was out of the running, a victim of a Pyrenees stage that could not have been more destructive and was ridden on a fiercely hot day.

The Tour entered a new era. Robert Millar, from the Peugeot team, exemplified the change, winning the stage in Luchon, while his teammate Pascal Simon took the yellow jersey.

Simon seemed strong enough to aim for Tour victory, but the next day he suffered a hairline fracture to his shoulder blade after a fall during the stage from Bagnères-de-Luchon to Roquefort. He would be forced to give up three days later.

The race was heading toward Alpe-d'Huez that particular day and Fignon picked up the scepter of the unlucky man from Troyes. All he had to do in this stage was fend off the two-headed attack from Jean-René Bernaudeau and Peter Winnen. The immense effort that he put into this struggle showed how well he had conserved his energy. The next day he had another hiccup on the Madeleine and Colombière passes. Fignon dropped behind by 4 minutes, but was able to remedy the situation with help from his teammates Madiot and Alain Vigneron.

The Tour was drawing to a close and Fignon had proved his growing worth, but had still not won a single stage, a fact that did not go unnoticed by the critics. He was

The first appearance of Laurent Fignon in the yellow jersey at the Tour de France in 1983. Hinault's absence cleared the way for other ambitious racers, with Fignon quickly rising to the forefront.

The Renault team started the 1984 Tour with huge ambitions and first-class riders: Greg LeMond (world champion) and Fignon (french champion). Both of them sought victory, but the team's unity would be preserved. Here, the two stars are led by teammate Pascal Jules.

Fignon pulled out all the stops to win in 1984. Scalded by an unfortunate experience in the Tour of Italy, where Moser had used his aerodynamic hour record bike, Fignon obtained a special bike from the Gitane R&D department.

TOUR DE FRANCE 1984

Fignon won his second Tour de France. He and Hinault were no longer teammates. But the Badger made life hard for him not allowing him a single moment of respite. Fignon was not the typical racing cyclist. He

made his own style, perfectly representing the young man of the 1980s. The bike was not everything for him, and when his career allowed him the time, he liked to go dancing and listen to music. France was split between Hinault and Fignon at the start of the 1984 Tour, but united behind them at the end, a state of affairs aptly summed up by a young boy's banner displayed during the last stage of the Tour: "Bravo Fignon and thanks Hinault!"

well aware of this though, which was why he made it a point of honor to win the time trial at Dijon. He just succeeded, beating runner-up Kelly by a split-second. Among the key riders he had to beat, Fignon defeated the Spaniard Angel Arroyo by half a minute, while Stephen Roche and Winnen were left 1:10 behind. In the final rankings, Arroyo, in second place, was 4:09 back. Fignon was far from being the winner of circumstance, which some liked to think. On the contrary, he was clearly the best of all those in the running. And everyone knew they hadn't heard the last of him.

The wait wasn't long. The young man from the Paris suburbs was in his golden years. He had just finished second in the 1984 Tour of Italy to Francesco Moser, who "stole" the race by using a cutting-edge bike in the final time trial. Fignon thus arrived at the start of the Tour the clear favorite.

Scalded by his unfortunate experience in the Giro, Fignon asked his bicycle constructor to study some new materials which, as they did for Moser, "help you win." The R&D department of Gitane, in Machecoul, certainly didn't waste any time and so the Delta bike was born, fitted with handlebars in the shape of a fin, and with flat tubes and streamlined parts.

The bike performed well in the prologue time trial at Noisy-le-Sec, with Fignon losing to Hinault by only 3 seconds. It was not particularly worrying for Fignon since 48 hours later he led a Renault team to victory in the team time trial. Marc Madiot, Fignon's teammate, won in Louvroil, and yearned to take the yellow jersey, but he would have to wait. He missed out by just a few seconds to the Dutchman Jacques Hanegraaf, ardent hunter of the bonus seconds that allowed various riders a slice of the cake. After Hanegraaf, it was the turn of Adri Van der Poel….

But the reign of Fignon's teammate Vincent Barteau lasted much longer, after he broke away in the chilly morning air of the stage from Bethune to Cergy-Pontoise in the company of Maurice Le Guilloux and the Portuguese Paolo Ferreira. The trio crossed the line 125 miles later with a lead of 17 minutes over the peloton. Barteau took the yellow jersey, an emblem that he was to keep until the Alps.

But while Hinault was starting to have some serious doubts, Fignon displayed a blissful optimism. He was in peak physical condition and the Renault team continued to accumulate stage victories…and Barteau's yellow jerseys.

So when the Alps came in sight, Fignon's supremacy had already been confirmed in the time trials. Then, in the Pyrenees he made an attack that earned him a sizeable time gap over Hinault. Final victory was once more in sight for the Renault rider.

At La Ruchère-en-Chartreuse, Fignon notched up another victory in the uphill time trial. Hinault avoided the KO, but saw himself being left a long way behind. He attempted to put some distance between himself and Fignon the next day on the Côte de Laffrey, which punctuated the stage from Grenoble to the Alpe-d'Huez. It barely seemed worth the effort as Fignon counterattacked and took off with Luis Herrera. The Badger still had some breath in him and he caught up with the two escapees before the attack on the Alpe-d'Huez. It was, however, his twilight hour, for he soon let go. Herrera took off like a condor, chasing the first Colombian stage victory in the Tour, and Fignon kicked off in turn, leaving Hinault adrift in their slipstream.

At the summit of the Alpe, where Herrera crossed

Tour de France 1986. Greg LeMond has taken the yellow jersey from Hinault after the seventeenth stage from Gap to Serre-Chevalier. But he knows that his teammate would take advantage of any mistake.

The Hinault-LeMond duo had some turbulent times during the 1986 Tour. The Breton promised the American that he would help him to win the Tour. But Hinault used nerve-racking tactics, by attacking LeMond in the Pyrenees, and doubt set in.

The start of the twentieth stage of the 1986 Tour, a time trial in Saint-Etienne. It seemed almost impossible for LeMond, yellow jersey, not to win the Tour, but Hinault had put such psychological pressure on him that he still doubted.

Hinault-LeMond, the devilish duo of the 1986 Tour. The two men finally decided to ride together instead of against each other. They would cross the finishing line of the Alpe-d'Huez stage side-by-side.

the line first, and where Fignon first earned the yellow jersey one year earlier, history repeated itself: The Parisian took the overall lead from his friend Barteau.

From now on, all that the Tour promised was the continued and unshaken domination of the yellow jersey; Fignon won again at La Plagne, Crans-Montana and in the time trial at Villefranche. On the Champs Elysées he took his second crown. Never again would he find the strength for such a performance. Quite simply, he had reached his peak.

Greg LeMond, the American exception

In 1986, Hinault promised his young teammate Greg LeMond that he would help him win the Tour de France, if he could prove himself capable. It was true that LeMond had been a great help in the Breton's 1985 Tour win.

But Hinault used tactics that completely flummoxed the American. On the twelfth stage from Bayonne to Pau, the 5-time Tour winner took the initiative with the complicity of his teammate Jean-François Bernard. Then, with 60 miles to go, the Spanish climbers Pedro Delgado and Eduardo Chozas joined the Hinault breakaway. On the Col de Marie-Blanque, the Breton rider increased the gap and, in Pau, took over the controls of the race with a 5:25 lead over LeMond, who had become a prisoner of the team race.

The next day, which included more major passes, Hinault—yes him again—accelerated during the descent of the Tourmalet. No one was able to follow him. Behind, LeMond still couldn't understand the Badger's tactics. The French maestro explained that he wanted to tire out his rivals at all costs, to wear them down so as to prepare the American's victory.

But Hinault wore himself down, and the ascent of the Col de Peyresourde saw Hinault starting to flounder. On the descent to Luchon, he was caught by Uro Zimmermann, Herrera, Millar and the two Americans LeMond and Andy Hampsten.

There remained the Superbagnères climb to the finish, and here LeMond took off and won the stage. Hinault still kept the yellow jersey by 40 seconds. The moment of truth would arrive in the Alps.

Arrived it certainly did, for in the seventeenth stage from Gap to the Col du Granon, via the Vars and Izoard passes, LeMond and Zimmermann went on the offensive. Hinault was suffering from a knee problem and LeMond took the yellow jersey.

The next day, another mountain stage, Hinault was

no longer in pain and, although it's not clear why, he decided to attack so as to show that he wasn't "dead." LeMond still didn't understand the Breton's game and panicked. Nevertheless, while Hinault and Zimmermann pranced on ahead, he was able to catch up with them thanks to the help of teammate Steve Bauer on the descent of the Galibier. LeMond and Hinault finally dumped Zimmerman on the Croix-de-fer climb, and were out on their own; they crossed the finish line together in Alpe-d'Huez. "A two-headed eagle," headlined *l'Equipe.*

The situation between the two men would remain tense right up until the end, but that didn't prevent LeMond from becoming the first American in history to win the Tour de France.

He would not content himself with this single victory.

The incredible reversal of 1989

At the start of the 1989 Tour, the favorite was Laurent Fignon. What could have been more logical? The Frenchman had just won the Tour of Italy. Who was there to challenge him? Greg LeMond had passed almost unnoticed in the Tour of Italy, although he had finished second in the final time trial behind the Pole Lech Piasecki. An interesting omen?

After a laborious first few days, the Tour reached its great individual test: the long time trial (45 miles) from Dinard to Rennes. Who were the forecasts favoring this time? Certainly Fignon. No one was in any doubt, although outside forces might well have a role to play. So it was that the

At the end of a Tour that had seen many twists and turns, Fignon, yellow jersey, lost the race by 8 seconds. Suffering a saddle-sore, he was beaten by an inspired LeMond. Here, Fignon has only a kilometer left in the Paris time trial, but he has already lost the Tour.

LeMond won the 1989 Tour after a dramatic and sensational conclusion. He won it by 8 seconds, the narrowest victory ever in Tour history.

They fought over LeMond with millions of francs after the 1989 Tour, with the Z team taking the booty and the 1990 Tour. The American won the yellow jersey following the time trial at Lac de Vassivière.

weather, excellent in the morning and stormy in the afternoon, would contribute to some surprising results. At any rate, the event marked the return of LeMond, who turned up on a bike fitted with triathlon-style handlebars. These gave him a better aerodynamic profile and four points to rest on: saddle, pedals, handlebars and armrests. However, the regulations foresaw only three resting points. But the race commissaires let it go. "How much did this innovation affect the final result of the Tour?" asked journalist Pierre Chany. An excellent question.

The result was there: LeMond won the stage by 24 seconds over another man making a comeback, Pedro Delgado, and most of all by 56 seconds over Fignon.

The American took the yellow jersey by 5 seconds.

A verdict was expected at the summit of Superbagnères, after a stage through the High Pyrenees. If Millar, Delgado and Charly Mottet had put themselves out of range of the other leaders, all the attention was focussed on the duel between LeMond and Fignon in the final climb.

About a mile from the finish, the American accelerated and the Frenchman counterattacked. LeMond made a great effort to catch up, but immediately blew. At the finish, Fignon had taken 12 seconds off him…and the yellow jersey. Justice had been served. But the Tour was far from over. What would the Alps bring?

LeMond took back the yellow jersey on the mountain time trial to Orcières-Merlette by taking 47 seconds out of Fignon. The American gained a further 14 seconds on the Gap-Briançon stage.

What were the prospects for the next day from Briançon to Alpe-d'Huez?

There was a savage struggle between LeMond, Fignon and Delgado. Two miles from the Alpe summit, Fignon attacked, giving it his all. Delgado tried to hang on and LeMond lost ground and only came back in the last two-thirds of a mile. By the top, he had ceded 1:19 to Fignon who, with a lead of 26 seconds now, retrieved the yellow jersey.

The gap between the two men was still minimal. Fignon knew this and attacked the next day on the Côte de Saint-Nizier, 2 miles from the summit and 16 miles from the finish in Villars-de-Lans. He won the stage and extended his overall lead by 14 seconds.

So 50 seconds separated Fignon from LeMond at the start of final-stage time trial from Versailles to the Champs-Elysées.

It would be a sensational and dramatic conclusion.

Fignon was suffering from an acute saddle-sore, which had first manifested itself in the nineteenth stage finish in Aix-les-Bains. The night before the final stage he hardly slept. He was pedaling lop-sidedly and in great pain.

Over the 16-mile individual time trial, he felt that he wasn't making any progress. He lost second after second …and was slowly losing the Tour.

LeMond won the Grande Boucle by 8 seconds—the narrowest gap ever recorded—at the expense of Fignon.

The American would win a third time, the following year, with the Z team. He arrived from the United States at the beginning of the season, in less than good condition, after a rather unsettled winter, which was not helped by a bout of glandular fever in April. Nobody in the cycling world thought that he could attain his previous levels of performance.

And yet, LeMond's Z team would back him up with a firm team spirit all through the Tour. After an admirable climb up the field, LeMond made a decisive attack in the Pyrenees, to put him in position to take the yellow jersey on the decisive time trial at the Lac de Vassivière.

Greg LeMond, three-time Tour winner.

Hinault had promised to help his teammate LeMond win the 1986 Tour. Here, at Alpe-d'Huez, the spectacle can be seen in all its glory. Almost too good to last…

LeMond's victory in the 1990 Tour was the victory of a whole team and the American's third Tour win. In three weeks, the Z company, the leading European manufacturer of children's clothes, boosted its public image by 28 percent.

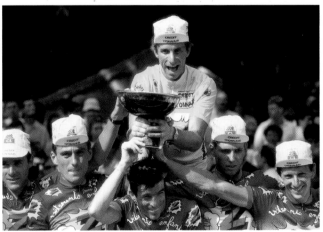

Miguel Indurain, "the Greatest Spaniard"

Indurain's first-ever appearance in yellow, in the 1991 Tour de France. Having escaped with Claudio Chiappucci, who would win at Val Louron in the Pyrenees, the Spaniard took the lead.

Opposite: Miguel Indurain. The Spaniard was the first member of the five-time Tour winner "club" to string all his wins together consecutively.

Mysterious, enigmatic Indurain, yellow jersey of the 1991 Tour. A man of amazing physiological capacities, his resting heart-rate was 28 beats per minute, his pulmonary capacity more than 8 liters and his pedaling power nearly 600 watts.

"Two hostesses helped him on with the yellow jersey. First of all the head, the yellow stitching sliding over his face. He closed his eyes and breathed deeply, inhaling the smell of this crown. He passed one arm through a sleeve, then the other, the jersey slowly rolling down the length of his torso, flooding him with light, knighting him, and his sweat mixed with the heroic sweat of past glories stuck to the jersey's fibers."

We owe these lines to Christian Laborde who, in his book on Miguel Indurain, tells of the first few minutes when the Spanish champion put on the yellow jersey of the Tour de France for the very first time.

It all happened on the second mountain stage in the Pyrenees, during the 1991 Tour, from Jaca to Val Louron. By chance, while climbing the Tourmalet, Indurain caught up with Greg LeMond who had broken away at the bottom of the pass. Indurain was accompanied by Luc Leblanc, yellow jersey, Gérard Rué, Andy Hampsten, Gianni Bugno, Mottet and Claudio Chiappucci.

Near the summit, everyone showed the effort on their faces. LeMond fell back and Indurain majestically accelerated, and disappeared into the descent.

On the slight incline of La Séoube, just before the Col d'Aspin, the Spaniard was warned by his team director that Chiappucci had just broken out of the group behind. He decided to wait. No one yet knew it, but the Tour was being decided right here.

Yet prior to this Tour, the encounters between Miguel Indurain and the Tour de France had not been without incident.

Apart from 1985, when his directeur sportif asked him to withdraw very early since he was still an "apprentice," he quit the race the following year before the Tour reached the Pyrenees. No one really understood what was up. He would explain later: "My father came to get me since he needed me at the farm. In fact, my team director José Miguel Echevarri only wanted me to complete the first twelve stages;

In the 1994 Tour, Indurain, whose future teammate Armand de Las Cuevas is seen setting the pace, slotted the final element of victory into place with his time trial win from Périgueux to Bergerac. After that, he managed both men and events with the intelligence, composure and experience that he was so well known for.

that was how it had been planned. But I was feeling good and I wanted to go further. So no doubt, fearing that I *would* go really far, he called my father and asked him to come and get me in Pau. I remember it well. I was in my pajamas when my father arrived. 'Come on,' he said, 'we're going home; I need you for the harvest.' So I got dressed, picked up my things and we returned to Villava by way of Arnéguy and Roncevaux. The Tour was over for me."

Indurian won the Tour five times. Apart from 1991, mentioned above, he also succeeded in winning the double Tour of Italy-Tour de France in 1992. That particular year, the Grande Boucle kicked off from San Sébastian, and Indurain started off by winning the prologue on Spanish soil. However, he soon left other riders to fight it out for the yellow jersey. He was even reproached for remaining in the shadow of the attackers—Chiappucci in particular, who in superb form, undertook an epic breakaway on the road to

Sestrière, over 6 major passes, including the Iseran. Indurain contented himself with finishing third in this thirteenth stage, knowing that he would take the yellow jersey. Above all, "Miguelon" realized the importance of that Tour's three time trial stages, including the prologue, in which he had excelled in great style.

A privileged spectator of the race, Bernard Hinault had several reservations: "Indurain is the best cyclist of his generation, but he won this Tour without any worries nor any great opposition. If his rivals continue to let him get away with it, there's a chance that his reign is going to last a while."

He wasn't wrong, for Indurain ran his race in exactly the same way the following year. Once again he won both the Tour of Italy and the Tour de France, showing himself to be clearly superior to the other riders, except for Tony Rominger, and without winning a single road stage.

He asserted himself from the very start of the 1993 Tour in the prologue at Puy-de-Fou in Vendée; and after that limited himself to managing his race in the style of a true conqueror, knowing that when the first big time trial arrived, at the Lac de Madine, he would again crush the opposition. And indeed that was where he finally won a stage—the ninth—leaving Bugno 2:11 behind him at the end of the 36-mile course.

From now on, having taken the yellow jersey, he contented himself with shadowing Rominger, whom he would beat in Serre-Chevalier, at Isola 2000 and during the last time trial, in Monthlhéry, without much trouble.

It was a fine piece of work carried out with great perceptiveness, but, as Pierre Chany would say, "without the audacity and those moments of self-motivation which enable the exceptional cyclist to rise above the common norms and to galvanize the crowds."

The years went by and Miguel Indurain continued his domination in the time trials.

In the 1994 Tour, the scenario again repeated itself during the ninth stage from Périgueux to Bergerac, a time trial; Indurain won it and left Rominger 2 minutes behind him. He thus took the yellow jersey, knowing that no one would come along and knock him off the leader position.

He did, however, demonstrate all of the finery of his jersey in the Pyrenees. Just before the ascent of Hautacam (a summit hitherto unexplored by the Tour and reached by a 7-mile climb), Indurain set an extremely fast, personal and steady pace. It was a strategy of total destruction. Only Richard Leblanc, Armand Virenque, de las Cuevas and

Tour de France 1994. Start of the final stage from Disneyland Paris to the Champs-Elysées. What better setting could one dream of for such a grand finale. Indurain certainly appreciated it.

Indurain based his whole season around the Tour de France, attracting the wrath of his compatriots for forsaking the Tour of Spain. However, his successes distanced him from such exaggerated feelings.

Just a few hundred yards more and Miguel Indurain would win his fifth Tour de France, of which he had been the absolute master since 1991. A permanent hegemony. At thirty-one years of age, he was at the height of his powers.

Marco Pantani were able to follow him, while the other favorites, such as Chiappuci and Rominger, were not able to answer the call.

About 1½ miles from the summit, Leblanc attacked the yellow jersey and managed to hold off the Spaniard at the finish line and win the stage. But nothing could shake the serenity of "King Miguel."

He mastered both men and events with intelligence and composure. And of course his great experience played a considerable role in his success.

Absolute master of the Tour since 1991, Indurain would win a fifth Tour de France in 1995.

This Tour was very nearly like the preceding ones, with one small difference: During the seventh stage from Charleroi to Liège, over the hilly roads of Liège-Bastogne-Liège, Indurain put on a most warlike show, with an attack that was as unpredictable as it was effective, taking only Johan Bruyneel with him in his wake. On that day, his rivals suffered a 50-second loss and severe trauma.

Opposite: Indurain ruled most of the time trials in which he took part during his five victorious Tours de France.

Indurain cut his way through the Tour de France a notch above everyone else. He set off on the Grande Boucle as one might go on stage, with an impressive naturalness and know-how. The Great Spaniard would remain invulnerable.

The first time trial was the very next day, on a tough course from Huy to Seraing. Would this again provide Indurain with the opportunity to fully assert his authority? Who could challenge him? The hierarchy fell into place once more, and Indurain set off to provide the perfect demonstration of how things should be done. This last victory of the man from Navarra proved to be a model of well-controlled power, intelligence and authority. Not a single tactical error, no volatile acts, nor slacking. "A nearly perfect Tour," affirmed Jean-Marie Leblanc, director of the Tour de France.

This was Indurain's last show. The following year he passed on the torch to the Dane Bjarne Riis. The Tour moved on into a new era, but one that was rather less conventional than the previous ones.

Wonderfully Absent

Poulidor, a true case of "Poupoularity"

Raymond Poulidor never wore the yellow jersey. Nevertheless, the word "Poulidorism" will no doubt one day be found in the dictionary. Over these next few pages we will discover the exact definition of the word.

Opposite: Tour de France 1962. Anquetil and Poulidor get up close and personal for the first time. An implacable rivalry was forming. To the left is the German Hans Junkermann.

"What he accomplished," wrote René Fallet, "he accomplished with his legs and his heart. Even though he was not the biggest star, at least he didn't cheat by being too big for his boots."

Raymond Poulidor enjoyed a popularity that withstood the test of time. The public eagerly identified with "Mr. Second Place," who couldn't quite overcome all of life's ups and downs.

But how many Frenchmen were as dogged, courageous and passionate as he? The writer Bernard Clavel summed up Poulidor's career as "a thousand victories that you won over yourself, as someone who never gives up."

But the attraction of such a mystery will always remain. A simple and honest man who came to embody a myth, "Poulidor the Unlucky" usually either crashed or wore himself out, lacking a strong team to confront the other's coalitions. Paradoxically, Poulidor was the absent yellow jersey par excellence. In fourteen Tours de France, the Limousin cyclist never wore the "golden fleece."

Jacques Goddet, in a special article in *l'Equipe*, covering the sixty years of the yellow jersey, pointed a reproachful finger at the emblem and addressed it thus: "Just one reproach my dear, old jersey, just one: why did you refuse Poupou so cruelly, brave among the brave, he who would have been most worthy of you?"

Even his Tour de France debut, as a young cyclist with the Mercier-BP team in 1962, was rather unfortunate.

Before the start was even in sight, he broke a pedal during his last training ride and found himself thrown to the ground. He stuck out his hand by pure reflex, to cushion his fall, and got it caught in the spokes, resulting in his arm needing to be plastered right up to the elbow. It was rather unlucky timing, to say the least. The legend of Poulidor the Unlucky had begun.

He decided to take the risk and turned up at the Nancy start. His courage was the source of much admiration, and many French people identified with him. As the stages passed, his fracture healed. He eventually found perfect form again and, feeling satisfied with his position, went on the offensive. Antonin Magne, his directeut sportif, tried to shake

"Poulidor the Unlucky"
(sixteenth stage from Font-
Romeu to Albi, 1968 Tour).

some reason into him: "Raymond, it's unthinkable that you should take part in the post-Tour criteriums as the injured man of the Tour de France. You're worth more than that. Prove it!"

On the stage from Briançon to Aix-les-Bains, through the Chartreuse mountains, Poulidor attacked in the steepest part of the Col de Porte. He was really set on doing something special.

He triumphed in Aix-les-Bains, with a 3 minute lead over Anglade and Bahamontes, climbing up to third place in the general classification, where he would remain. This performance won him the hearts of the crowd, who all firmly believed that he would one day win the Tour, or at least the yellow jersey.

The following year saw the second missed rendezvous with the yellow jersey. But he showed his stuff, coming second in the Angers time trial, 45 seconds behind Jacques Anquetil. The press could not help but note the great promise in the young rider.

In 1964, the implacable rivalry between Anquetil and Poulidor reached its peak, with the two men crossing swords for the entire season. When their paths separated, Poulidor went off to win the Tour of Spain and Anquetil the Tour of Italy.

An explosive Tour de France was expected.

The two stars fought each other second for second, but Poulidor made a few tactical errors, still not able to take advantage of the others' little mistakes; in Monaco, for instance, on the cinder track finish, he mistakenly calculated which lap he was on.

With the Alps behind them, nothing had yet been decided. Anquetil was still the time trial king, but the judgment of the Pyrenees was still to come.

On the stage from Andorra to Toulouse, Anquetil paid dearly for his overeating the previous rest-day. His laborious start put him 4 minutes behind Poulidor and Bahamontes at the summit of the Col d'Envalira. But the marvelous "Anquetil machine" finally got fired up in the descent and the gap decreased, until he caught Poulidor's group 43 miles from the finish. Poulidor had had his chance. Everything was left to race for again, and Poulidor came up short when he suffered an untimely mechanical problem. Two minutes and 52 seconds now separated him from Anquetil in the general classification.

Poulidor attacked the next day, in the first bends of the Col du Portillon. He was invincible. At the finish, in Luchon, he beat the Anquetil peloton by 1:16.

But misfortune would not let go of its prey. In the time trial from Peyrehorade to Bayonne, the man whom the French familiarly nicknamed "Poupou" was held up by a puncture. Anquetil, yellow jersey, was now leading Poulidor by 56 seconds.

The arrival at the summit of the Puy-de-Dôme was Poulidor's last chance. The Tour was about to live one of its most famous episodes; the most dramatic stage ever as far as intensity was concerned.

Over the last 3 miles, just when he seemed to be unbeatable, Anquetil cracked. Even so, right up to the last mile he parried Pouluidor blow for blow, trying to hide his anxiety under an impenetrable mask. The image of the two men side by side is legendary.

The Limousin accelerated again and again. Anquetil could do nothing but grit his teeth, watching his rival ride away through the dense and frenetic crowds. At the summit, Poulidor's name was on everyone's lips as they urged him on. When he crossed the line, he was just 14 seconds short of snatching the yellow jersey from the Norman.

Poulidor never won the yellow jersey. But he became part of a legend so beautiful it will never be forgotten.

The Puy-de-Dôme (1964 Tour). The Anquetil-Poulidor duel had now reached mythic proportions.

Opposite: The glow of a mystery would linger on, that which turned a simple and honest man into a myth.

Anquetil-Poulidor: France was torn between them.

There remained a time trial from Versailles to Paris, but there was no way Poulidor could make up time against his rival, the all-powerful master of this specialty.

Poulidor eventually lost the Tour by 55 seconds, but his popularity had reached its peak.

In 1965, Anquetil didn't take part in the Tour de France. Surely this would leave the way open for Poulidor? Unfortunately, his path was blocked by a young man from Bergamo, Felice Gimondi, to whom he would concede a minute in the stage from Liege to Roubaix, after a crash, then 2 minutes the next day in the stage from Roubaix to Rouen.

Victorious in the time trial, Poulidor really woke up on Mont Ventoux, breaking away with the Spaniard Julio Jimenez. Everyone thought that he would finally take the yellow jersey, but Gimondi made a superhuman effort, broke away from Jan Janssen, Guido De Rosso and Jean-Claude Lebaube and caught up with Henri Anglade, whom he clung onto like a lifejacket. Thanks to a steady pace set by Anglade, the young Italian kept his golden tunic by just 34 seconds. Poulidor had missed another chance.

In 1966, Poulidor succumbed to the force of the

Anquetil-Aimar coalition, with the former helping his teammate to shake off Poulidor. He was trapped again.

It is clear that based solely on the basis of popularity he should have won the yellow jersey. His fame was based on that universal dialectic of the physical clashing of opposing forces and the opposition of good and evil.

He failed once again in the 1967 Tour, even though Anquetil was now absent. He just missed taking the yellow jersey in the prologue, which was taken by the Spaniard Errandonea by just 6 seconds. Repeatedly ensnared in the first few stages, he knew that he had already lost the Tour, but declared that he would help his French teammate Roger Pingeon. Pingeon duly won, and Poulidor got another boost for his popularity.

The following year, Poulidor's misfortune was back in strength, when he was obliged to withdraw, after a crash, in the stage from Font-Romeu to Albi.

In January 1969, *Miroir du cyclisme* splashed Raymond Poulidor right across the cover, with the headline: "1969, the yellow dream." But a new star was rising fast: Eddy Merckx.

In the prologue of the 1969 Tour, the yellow jersey floated just 22 seconds out of Poulidor's reach, to land on the back of Rudi Altig. But everyone's dreams were soon dispatched by Merckx.

Though born on April 15, 1936, Poulidor refused to be beaten by age, and in 1973 had never been so close to the golden fleece. In the prologue, which was held in Scheveningen, not far from the Hague, Joop Zoetemelk took the yellow jersey on home ground, but he was only 80/100ths of a second in front of Poulidor. And so, for less than a second, Poupou failed to win one of the few great cycling honors that were still missing from his collection: the famous yellow jersey.

Commenting on his turbulent record he once said: "I do wonder whether I would not prefer popularity born of a great triumph as opposed to popularity born of misfortune, if only to feel the difference!"

He finished third in his last Tour, in 1976.

"What he accomplished," wrote René Fallet, "he accomplished with his legs and his heart. Even though he was not the biggest star, at least he didn't get too big for his boots. Don't laugh at this boy. Smile at him. Subtlety. When he hangs up his cleats, say of him: 'He was clean, he was honest.'"

5

Up There
on the Mountain

Jean Robic, the man who outblew the wind

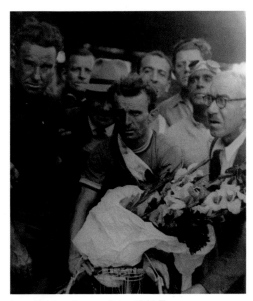

Jean Robic, winner of the 1947 Tour.

Previous page: Charly Gaul and Federico Bahamontes climbing together. The enchantment begins. Each had his own style; Gaul capered, while Bahamontes preferred more deliberate pedal strokes.

Opposite: The "Breton Elf," an aggressive, tenacious, winged climber. All of France cried "Go Robic!" as soon as the rider's silhouette appeared.

Assisted by Gaston Monnerville, Robic puts on his only yellow jersey of the 1967 Tour, that of the last day which brought him final victory.

The year 1947 saw the return of the Tour after World War II. The event was eagerly awaited by the public, as well as by a certain Jean Robic, a Breton from Morbihan, who had come to the forefront the previous year in the Monaco-Paris race, a sort of mini-Tour de France.

The French team had slammed the door in his face, though, and so he took refuge with the West France regional team. He was married a few days before the start, to Raymonde, a young woman whose parents owned *Au rendez-vous des Bretons,* a bar situated just next to the Montparnasse station in Paris. It was a bit bizarre to get married just before the Tour, but Robic had a ready answer: "Impossible, a wedding at the dawn of the Tour? Well, we shall see. I've staked everything on this race. I've been criticized. It has been said that my defeats this season have been due to bad health, and poor form. See you at the start and…we'll see."

The morning after his wedding night, he was up at 7 o'clock to knock off a few miles on his bike.

The Tour left Paris and all eyes were soon fixed on another frenchmen, René Vietto, who took the yellow jersey on the second stage. But Robic, too, showed his form was good by winning in Strasbourg on the fourth day.

Fully confidant, he wrote to his mother: "It's certainly a surprise, and one that will make you very happy. I now hope to offer you final victory at the Parc des Princes"

On the road, he again proved himself to be the man of the Alps, winning in Grenoble. He left everyone behind on the climbs, to take the stage on his own.

He did, however, run into some bad luck in the Briançon stage, where he was held back by numerous punctures. Vietto took the yellow jersey, with Robic now 18 minutes behind.

Was the Tour to be decided in the Pyrenees? Robie's best chance came on the stage from Pau to Luchon, over the highest passes. At the start, the ex-winner of the Tour,

Vietto, French idol before the war, had lost nothing of his popularity when the Tour started again in 1947. His pupil "Apo" Lazarides stands near him.

Opposite: Charly Gaul during the time-trial ascent of Mont Ventoux. In spite of his success on this stage, everyone thought that the Tour was lost for him. This didn't take into account the rain and storms that would assist him to transcend the race a few days later (1958 Tour).

Robic, yellow jersey for a day for the second time (1953 Tour). He would pass on his trophy to his teammate François Mahé.

Georges Speicher, shouted out to him sharply: "Hey, Robic, what are you going to do today?"

"I'll break away from the start and finish on my own," Robic shouted back in a high, clear voice.

The whole caravan already called him "Biquet," a nickname given to him by his teammate Eloi Tassin, who had started off by calling him "Robiquet."

The Breton began his attack as soon as they left Luchon. Breaking away with him were Apo Lazarides, Primo Volpi, René Vietto and Pierre Brambilla. Robic continued to accelerate on the Peyresourde climb, and his companions fell back one by one.

"I thought about Raymonde my wife," he recounted, "about my little mother. I imagined them standing by a tree at the end of the road, urging me on, and so I sprinted toward them. Then I said to myself: 'No, they're further on!' and this little game with my imagination carried on indefinitely, obliging me to go faster and faster."

In the following cars, two great Tour winners, André Leducq and Sylvère Maës took off their caps as they went past him, saluting the Breton with a hearty and considerate "Monsieur Robic."

The Pau finish was soon in sight. He swept across the line, taking nearly 11 minutes off Vietto, to which were added 4 bonus minutes on the passes and a bonus minute for the finish. He now stood at 8:08" from "King René."

"Nothing is lost yet," he cried. "I can feel it, I am unbeatable!"

But nothing major happened again until the time-trial stage from Vannes to Saint-Brieuc: 86 miles. They crossed Brittany from one coast to the other. The day before, the riders had had a rest day in Vannes, when Robic received a visit from his wife and grandmother. He describes the scene in his own picturesque way: "In the hotel, I slept next to my wife. Nothing could be more normal or healthy…. In a room with twin beds I should point out. I switched off the light. Raymonde switched it back on. I told her to switch it back off. She eventually did, but started to whistle with a trill in her throat like a lovesick turtledove…. This was too much! I exploded, shouting, 'Are you going to stop or what?' And I gave her a poke which clearly wasn't one of tenderness. We finally got to sleep, her on her side and me on mine. First priority was the yellow jersey. In Paris, after the finish, we would have all the time in the world for such messing about."

The next day, Robic set out across his home territory. 86 miles on his own against the clock. Quite a trek, particularly along hilly back roads, including the ascent of the famed Mur de Bretagne.

One sensed that he was rather tense at the start. He had filled his water bottle up to the brim: two-thirds roasted barley and one-third Calvades brandy.

Carried along by the delirious crowd, he slowly gnawed away at the lead of the Belgian Raymond Impanis, who would win the stage. Robic finished in second place and moved up to third place in the general classification behind Brambilla, the new yellow jersey. "Biquet" was now just 2:58 behind the Italian from Annecy.

Everything would be played out on the final day's stage from Rouen to Paris.

Upon leaving Rouen, on the Côte de Bonsecours, Robic saw Brambilla stuck in the middle of a group. By reflex, the little Frenchman sped off on the cobbles, which were smooth as a mosaic, and broke clear. Brambilla managed to catch up, Robic let him approach and then broke away again. Brambilla caught up again. Taking advantage of all the confusion, Fachleitner, of the French team, counterattacked him again. Brambilla set off after him. But he had already overstretched himself and was unable to bridge the gap. Robic now took over the reins and set off after Fachleitner, whom he caught at the summit of the hill. The two men set off together for a long trek that would finish in the Parc des Princes with final Tour de France victory for Robic.

"I will always remember myself in Ville-d'Avray," Robic recounted. "As much as I tried to stop myself dreaming, I was already completing my lap of honor with the bouquet in my arms. I stood up on the pedals, tensed my arms and thighs, while repeating to myself: 'It's you who's going to win.'"

Charly Gaul, "the Angel of the Mountains"

Charly Gaul was a phenomenon in the cycling world. He gobbled up the mountain roads with his jerky pedaling style and "asthmatic gear ratio." Whoever saw the Luxembourger climb, saw the best, the most beautiful and uplifting climber on record.

He was a strange character. He liked neither to laugh nor cry, disliked journalists and photographers, and could not stand the heat. But he surely liked bad weather, since his greatest exploits were carried off in the worst conditions. On the other hand, it must be remembered that in 1958, on the sun-drenched slopes of Mont Ventoux, he won a time trial that thrust him to the forefront of a Tour de France that he would eventually conquer…in the rain.

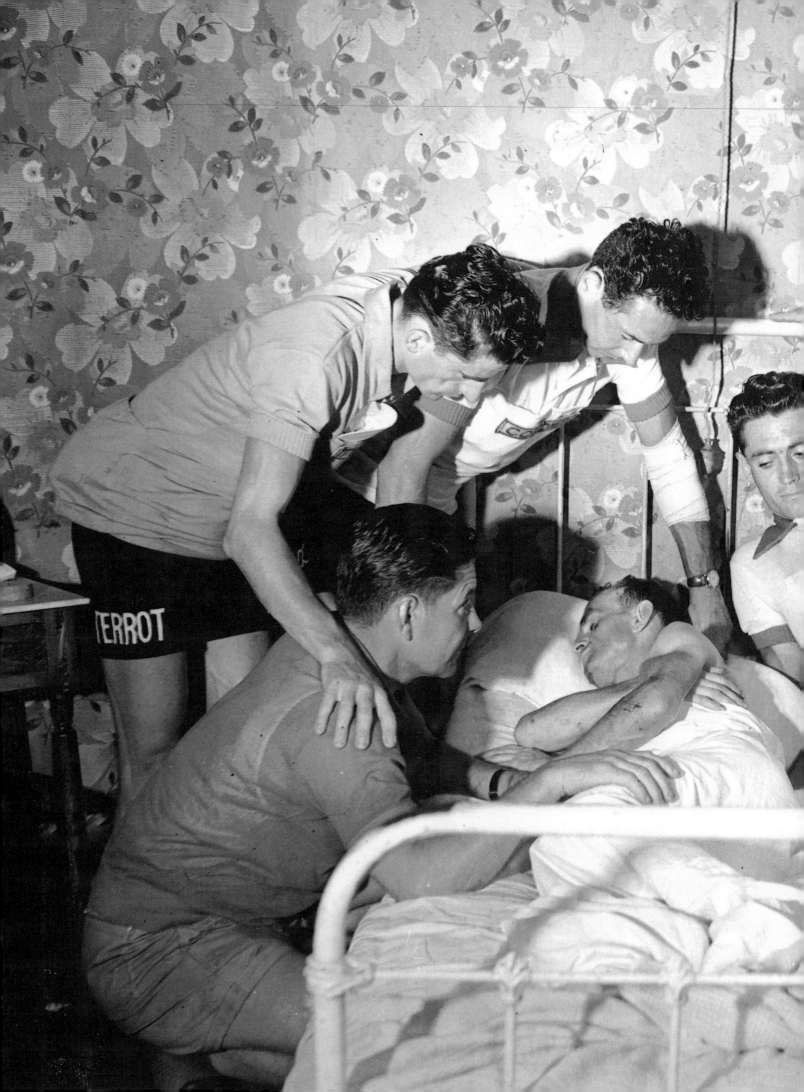

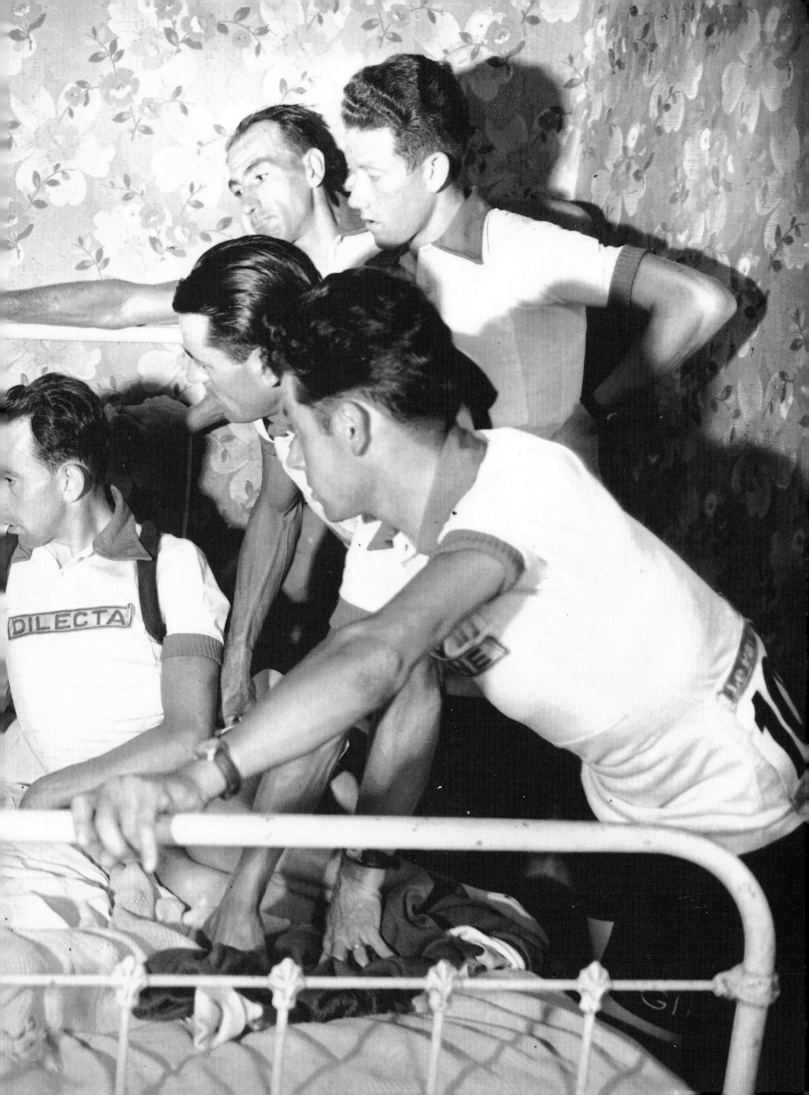

The 1961 Tour. Anquetil, yellow jersey from the first day to the last, dominated the entire race. Nobody dared to attack him. The passes were climbed at a steady pace. Jacques Goddet spoke of "the Dwarves of the Road." Even Gaul and Imerio Massignan, in the lead here, seemed resigned to it.

Previous pages: Drama on the 1953 Tour. Robic, injured, cannot carry on. His teammates gather in his hotel room to say good-bye. Left to right: Malléjac (yellow jersey), Chupin, F. Mahé, Morvan, Pontet, Bultel, Audaire and Esnault. Kneeling: The directeur sportif Léon Le Calvez.

In that Tour de France, Gaul proved also to be the time-trial king, even though that meant he had to beat Jacques Anquetil. The defending champion knew that the opening time trial stage—which took place over 29 miles on the selective Circuit de L'Aulne at Châteaulin—would be important, and forecast: "He who wins tomorrow will win the Tour de France." The forecast would prove to be most accurate. It must be said that the course fitted Gaul like a glove, with the climb of Stang-ar-Garront. Anquetil, who placed second to Gaul, didn't seem to be on top form. In fact, during the twentieth stage, he had breathing problems and reached Aix-les-Bains half an hour behind the leaders. He didn't start the next day.

In order to understand Charly Gaul, one must understand that he was a great cyclist from a small country. In that era of national teams, he paid dearly for this, riding with hybrid teams for a long time, since Luxembourg was unable to form a really good Tour team of its own. So Gaul, in spite of his talent, always found himself doomed when faced with better structured teams. He was teamed with Austrians, Germans, Portuguese, English... Poor Charly! He might climb well to the summit of passes and win time trials, but his talent would never bloom within these multinational teams.

In 1958, a miracle happened! Luxembourg found itself associated with the powerful Dutch team, which included Piet Damen, Wim Van Est, and Geerit Voorting. The men from the Grand-Duchy, apart from Gaul, were Marcel Ernzer, Jempy Schmitz and Aldo Bolzan. Finally they could bring their "Angel of the Mountains" to the fore.

From the very first stages, many of the riders were on high alert, particularly the Belgian Jean Brankhart, a race favorite, who confided, though it was hardly necessary, to his directeur sportif Jean Aerts: "The riders of the French team seem rather disinterested in Charly Gaul for the moment. What a mistake! Watch out, if they let him reach the foot of the passes with the same overall time as the top favorites. He only has to let himself be carried along by Wim Van Est and the other Dutchmen on the flat, just to limit the damage; after that he'll be virtually untouchable, because the best climber, that's him!"

On the third day, Wim Van Est was determined to show his teamleader Gaul that he was in no way prepared to play second fiddle. He took the yellow jersey, while Gilbert Bauvin won the stage. The next day, it would be the latter's turn to wear the yellow jersey, but the day after that, in Brittany at the Saint-Brieuc finish, it was taken by another Dutchman, Geerit Vooring. Amazing Voorting, who immediately felt a strong stirring of emotion for his wife.

Shortly before the start of the Tour, the couple had actually made a record where they both sang a martial song, "All for the Yellow Jersey." The record was already a hit, from Amsterdam to the Hague. On one side, Voorting and his wife mixed their voices in a charming duet that was as much a profession of faith, while on the other side, Van Est and Wout Wagtmans sung along to this innocent refrain.

What a miracle of will: after seven days of racing, Van Est and Voorting had succeeded in bringing the yellow jersey back to their hotel four times.

The following day brought a fresh miracle: Voorting succeeded in hanging on to his leader's position, in spite of the time trial. He fought across the Châteaulin course with such an iron will, that he was able to keep a slim 3-second lead over Frenchman François Mahé in the general classification, but everyone could feel that the serious business was only just beginning.

As dictated by tradition, the yellow jersey started last in the time trial. But Voorting arrived early to warm up…and brought along a record-player. On it, he placed his piece of chart-breaking vinyl! Charly listened and grinned.

A delicate shiver ran through Gaul's forearms and he sped away. Over the 29 miles of the circuit he literally surpassed himself. From the team car, his directeur sportif Jean Goldschmidt, with his megaphone held high, advised him which gears to use. For Charly and his teammates this was the start of their coup d'état.

Bahamontes showed his determination by winning the fourteenth stage from Pau to Luchon, and on Mont Ventoux the king was clearly Gaul. But he didn't have the yellow jersey and, after all, was he really such a sure bet? These

In 1955, a young man from Luxembourg gave Bobet quite a scare. Gaul would have to wait three long years for Tour victory.

Gaul's thoracic capacity appears to be quite impressive! His teammates Jempy Schmitz and Marcel Ernzer seem to agree.

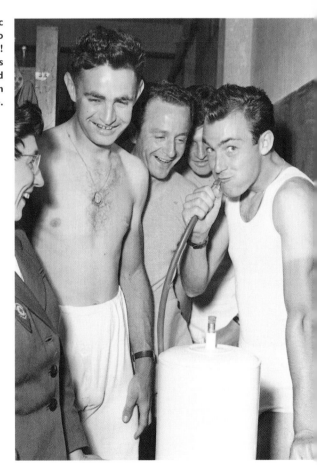

With his torso held high, and the face of a tragic actor, this was the climber that the whole of Spain was waiting for: Federico Bahamontes (wearing the yellow jersey, in 1963).

doubts were emphasized the next day, from Carpentras to Gap, when he dropped behind by 11 minutes. Bahamontes appeared to be a much safer bet, and on the Gap-Briançon stage he proved himself the master of the Izoard and took the stage. Then, on the following day, everything changed, on the stage from Briançon to Aix-les-Bains. On July 16, Gaul realized the supreme exploit. At the start, upon leaving the hotel, the riders were lashed by an icy rain. All of them felt oppressed by these awful conditions, except Charly Gaul, the man for all weather.

He now became a true "assassin" of his rivals. Without getting out of the saddle, he spun his small gear, gliding across the summits of the Chartreuse, shrugging off the cold rain that never stopped. An exceptional climber, Gaul managed to form a calm aura around himself in these apocalyptic surroundings. He crossed the finish line in Aix-les-Bains, beating the Belgian Adriaenssens by 8 minutes, the Italian Favero by 10 minutes and the yellow jersey, Géminiani, by nearly a quarter of an hour.

Although Favero took the yellow jersey, it was only temporary, since Gaul won the time trial from Besançon to Dijon and became the uncontested conqueror of the Tour de France. The Tour had finally smiled on Gaul.

Federico Bahamontes; "the Eagle of Toledo"

If one had to pick an essential characteristic of Federico Martin Bahamontes, then it would be his ability to climb passes faster than anyone, just as he descended them slower than anyone. This hidalgo, who seemed just as proud as all hidalgos, attempted to show himself as humble as possible in his approach to things. He was crazy, but crazy with genius. When seeing him arrive at the 1954 Tour de France, pedaling with an upright torso and a face set as if on the Road to Calvary, one could have been forgiven for wondering if this was really the winged climber that the Spanish had chosen to relay the torch of victory from Jesus Loroño Arteaga. But after the first few climbs there was no longer any doubt. Bahamontes was clearly the new king of the mountains and everyone was astonished by his various high-jinks. Could one ever forget how, in his first Tour de France, he took the Col de Romeyère in the lead, only to stop a few meters further on to savor a vanilla ice cream!

He had the emaciated face of the dead gypsy characterized by another Federico, Spain's great poet, Garcia Lorca. Bahamontes's hair was curly and his teeth pearly white. Bursting with life, he knew no greater happiness than riding

Bahamontes has just put on the yellow jersey in Grenoble (1959 Tour). He would keep it to the end.

out on his own with nothing but sky and emptiness around him, along the rock-covered roads, his shoulders cloaked in mountain fog.

He had that intrinsic class that sets men of excellence apart, but he often wasted it in spontaneous bursts, forgetting that a Tour victory is built from carefully measured steps, if not calculations. He would, however, win this victory in 1959.

The short but treacherous ascents of the Massif Central, climbed in a heatwave during the thirteenth stage from Albi to Aurillac, delivered a hearty knock to many riders, including Louison Bobet and Charly Gaul, who finished 20 minutes behind the stage winner, Henry Anglade. The French champion had broken away with Anquetil, Bahamontes and Britain's first Tour star, Brian Robinson.

After the wonderful victory of André Le Dissez in Clermont-Ferrand, came the Puy-de-Dôme time trial, where Bahamontes caught fire. His victory brought him to just 4 seconds from the yellow jersey, worn by the Belgian Hoevenaers. He would eventually take it from him on the great alpine stage from Saint-Etienne to Grenoble, which he finished in second place, behind an inspired Gaul.

Frenchman Roger Rivière had already lost the Tour by dropping 4 minutes behind in the Aurillac stage. This did not stop him, however, from winning the final time trial from Seurre to Dijon.

After the eighteenth stage, from Grenoble to Aoste, it was clear that Bahamontes had won the Tour. He certainly benefited from the neutrality of the French team, which wished to prevent the victory of a regional champion at all costs, in this case Anglade, while Anquetil and Rivière had only one thing on their minds: wearing the other down. At the Parc des Princes, where Bahamontes savored his triumph, Anglade finished second, while Anquetil (third) led Rivière (fourth).

This was the Norman's only ambition and the crowd at the Parc des Princes, who understood this only too well, whistled and booed him as loud as they could. The bitter taste of this reception would remain in Anquetil's mouth for many years and he even named his boat *Sifflets 59* (Whistles 59).

"It was due to his nifty footwork over the French mountains," wrote Jean Bobet, "that this proud hidalgo became the first cycling matador of his country."

But how could one resent this eccentric Iberian who was always missing some part or other of his cycling equipment. A wheel here, a track bike there, a pair of shoes, or tights… He was a mercenary cyclist, defending the prestige of a brand of aperitif in Italy, promoting the qualities of a coffee machine

"The Eagle of Toledo" soars away on the ascent of the Puy-de-Dôme in the 1959 Tour. The whimsical Bahamontes became the number one pretender to final victory.

Bahamontes, in his first Tour de France in 1954; the slopes of the Pyrenees revealed a hitherto unknown climber.

Lucien Van Impe would win the King of the Mountains title ever year he rode in the Tour. Then his ambition increased a notch (1976 Tour).

Van Impe wins the Pla-d'Adet stage and takes the yellow jersey. At the end of his eighth Tour he finally won it (1976).

in Spain, those of a cycle manufacturer in Switzerland, or the shine of a toothpaste in France. Nobody found this unnatural, for he was Bahamontes after all, wonderfully mysterious, relaxed, proud and jealous, who preferred to play the role of "the Toledo Harlequin" in order to gain popular favor. He did nothing like anyone else, including his use of language, a kind of compendium of expressions that he had picked up by crossing borders. "This crazy Fédé", as Jean Bobet called him.

Lucien Van Impe's Tour

The Belgian Lucien Van Impe appeared to have a lifetime subscription to the King of the Mountains title, having won it three times in a row when he started the 1976 Tour.

"A mountainous Tour", and "A Tour tailor-made for the climbers"…such were the comments of the press. And there was one essential characteristic: The Alps and Pyrenees were separated by just one transition stage, in Manosque, from where the riders were taken by plane to Port-Baracrès. Also. the riders were offered no fewer than five summit finishes.

However, this 1976 Tour was certainly wide open. Eddy Merckx had declined to take part, following the advice of his doctors, because of a saddle sore that required surgery. As for Bernard Thévenet, the previous year's winner, he didn't appear to have the right form for a new success, in spite of his victory in the Dauphiné Libéré.

The bookies' favorites were clearly Joop Zoetemelk, still lying in wait, and little Lucien Van Impe, if he could finally muster some ambition and stop limiting himself to his area of predilection, the mountains prize. But since the mountains comprised the plat de résistance, then perhaps he could do it. Why not?

It should be noted that, until now, the Belgian had hardly benefited from a favorable team. Nifty little climber that he was, he always devoted himself to becoming King of the Mountains, and so when he set out to attack the passes on his own he lacked teammates who were up to his standard—except perhaps in 1975 with Alain Santy and Mariano Martinez, although they were not in great condition that year.

There was an important change in the 1976 Gitane-Campagnolo team, with Cyrille Guimard succeeding Jean Stablinski as directeur sportif. The ex-racer from Nantes immediately set to work to instill some team spirit in his men. It had become imperative that Van Impe was properly supported, since the Tour was also fought out on the flat. The climber had finally understood this, and so no one was surprised when, at the start of the race, Van Impe declared: "I'm starting this Tour to win it."

Another Belgian, Freddy Maertens, started off the Tour in glorious style. But Van Impe just watched him, eagerly awaiting the mountains.

From Saint-Jean-de-Monts, the race headed toward Belgium and reached its first mountainous section during the ninth stage from Divonne-les-Bains to Alpe-d'Huez.

From now on it was up to Van Impe to make his play. It was his role to bring back the notion of the lightweight cyclist who ensures his effectiveness through smooth pedaling.

The Norman Raymond Delisle was the first to make an attack, and it was just what Van Impe and Zoetemelk had been waiting for. The Belgian and the Dutchman very quickly took the lead. Zoetemelk, who was a faster sprinter than Van Impe, won the stage, but acrobatic Lucien took his first yellow jersey.

The same thing happened the next day, in Montgenèvre, where Zoetemelk won the stage, leading a close-knit pack of seventeen riders.

Very soon they came to the Pyrenees, with Pyrenees 2000 reached by way of the Aussières and Jau passes. Once again it was an offensive by Delisle that drew them on. Van Impe bided his time, observing Guimard's prudent advice. Zoetemelk was suffering from a saddle abscess and so Delisle won this first Pyrenees stage without too much trouble and took the yellow jersey. The peloton of favorites lost about seven minutes and Van Impe found himself in second place, 2:04 behind the Peugeot rider.

Everyone thought that the Tour would be settled two days later, during the stage from Saint-Gaudens to Pla-d'Adet, over the Menté, Portillon and Peyresourde passes. Van Impe no longer had any choice. He had to attack Delisle and take the yellow jersey from him, while affording Zoetemelk no chance of getting back in the hunt. As for Thévenet, in bad form and sick, the Tour was already lost.

Riding in one of the lead groups containing all of the favorites, Van Impe triggered the battle in the Col du Portillon; Delisle and Zoetemelk were hesitant about chasing after him and stared questioningly at each other.

In the valley, various groups were forming in front, and Van Impe found himself alongside Ocaña, Jean-Pierre Danguillaume, Giuncarlo Bellini and José Pesarrodona, among others.

In the long ascent of the Peyresourde, Zoetemelk, who was lagging 2 minutes behind, finally decided to chase after Van Impe. He broke away from Delisle, but it was already too late.

On the slopes of the pass, the Belgian benefited from

The most number of yellow jerseys by Tour de France

8 jerseys: 1987.
7 jerseys: 1951, 1962, 1968, 1978, 1998.
6 jerseys: 1929, 1931, 1937, 1949, 1953, 1959, 1966, 1967, 1983, 1984, 1995.

The least number of yellow jerseys by Tour de France

1924: 1 (Bottecchia)
1920: 1 (Frantz)
1935: 1 (R. Maës)
1921: 2 (Mottiat, Scieur)
1934: 2 (Magne, Speicher)
1961: 2 (Anquetil, Darrigade)
1970: 2 (Merckx, Zilioli)
1972: 2 (Merckx, Guimard)
1977: 2 (Thévenet, Thurau)
1999: 2 (Armstrong, Kirsipuu)

Van Impe (center) often contented himself with his best climber jersey. He did not, however, have the slightest complex when faced with riders like Gimondi, Thévenet, Zoetemelk and Merckx (left to right).

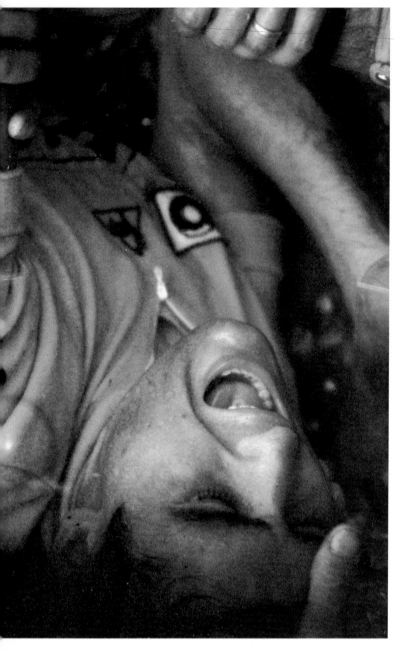

THE PAIN OF LUIS OCAÑA

Ocaña has just crashed out of the Tour in a storm of unbelievable violence that had burst just a few minutes before. "The Pyrenees were prisoners of a somber wedding feast," wrote Paul Katz. The yellow jersey lay there, bleeding, at the side of the road (1971 Tour).

the sturdy support of Ocaña; the Spaniard let rip and the combined efforts of the two men condemned Zoetemelk, who too was pushing himself to the limit, but all on his own.

Van Impe, forcing his accelerations and changes of rhythm on his breakaway partner, soon found himself out on his own on the slope of Pla-d'Adet. He won the stage and took back the yellow jersey. Zoetemelk found himself second overall, 3:12 behind Van Impe.

Everything finally was right for Van Impe in his eighth Tour. He could now fulfill his childhood dream: to get up close to wild animals during a photo-safari in Kenya. He also built himself a villa, no longer in Mere, where he was born on the October 20, 1946, but 3 miles away in…Impe!

Luis Ocaña, blood and lightning

In the 1971 Tour de France, Luis Ocaña's crash, while wearing the yellow jersey, reverberated through the race caravan like a thunderclap. The next day, in *l'Equipe,* Antonin Blondin wrote: "Luis Ocaña was perhaps not intrinsically the best in the race, but he was the shining star, forming, with the sun, an inseparable couple, whose complementary heat and illumination had been dazzling us for four days. All it took was twenty minutes of overcast sky over the Pyrenees for a brief cyclone, of cataclysmic proportions, to sweep our beautifully flashing blade to the ground, just when he was preparing to crown himself on his native soil and his favorite stamping ground, for our greatest pleasure."

At the start of the 1971 Tour, Merckx still held center stage. He remained the great favorite, after having already twice won the Grande Boucle. But Ocaña finally showed himself ready to contest this supremacy.

As the Tour headed toward the center of France, the Spaniard wished to "tease" Merckx in the stage that finished at the summit of the Puy-de-Dôme. The Belgian led the Spaniard by 52 seconds in the general classification.

For Ocaña and his Bic team, the tactic was simple: isolate Merkx, by cutting him off from his teammates during the final climb. One of the Bic team, Bernard Labourdette, would attack from the foot of the climb so as to scatter everyone. It would then be Ocaña's turn to go into action.

The plan was followed. Merckx, though tired, chased anything that broke away. When Thévenet attacked in turn, Merckx duly went after him and Ocaña judged this the opportune moment to launch his own offensive. He passed everyone and went on to win the stage, 15 seconds ahead of Merckx. The first part of the Bic team's strategy had worked well.

Luis Ocaña, a true toreador.

Two days later, between Saint-Etienne and Grenoble, the Belgian champion had a stroke of extreme bad luck. He got a puncture during the descent of the Cucheron. Thévenet, Zoetemelk and Gösta Petterson jumped away, taking Ocaña with them, and Merckx had lost sight of the leading men for good. Ocaña soon took the lead of his group and his devastating power saw the others gasping in his wake. At the finish he was passed by the others in the sprint, with Zoetemelk taking the yellow jersey, but Ocaña was the hero of the day.

The time had now come for the big battle that Ocaña so desired. That evening, at dinner, he predicted: "This is it. The Cannibal is ripe."

The next day, the stage from Grenoble to Orcières-Merlette crossed the Dévoluy, an arid land with no shade and a disheartening gradient, in torrid heat. They would have a tough climb to 5459 feet, with another climb to the finish in Orcières-Merlette—at 5962 feet a new summit in the Tour.

The Portuguese Joaquim Agostinho opened the hostilities. Ocaña chased after him, with Zoetemelk, Van Impe and Petterson responding, having understood that the fateful hour had arrived. Merckx lost contact. A moment of pathos. Agostinho was caught by the pursuers and they formed a new group; but Ocaña was not content to stay there. He put on a fantastic display of power, emanating from his smooth pulls. Nothing interrupted his harmonious movement.

One could not say the same of his breakaway companions, subdued by each pedal stroke. At this pace, he was soon out on his own. At the foot of the Col du Noyer, Merckx was already 3 minutes behind.

Soon the tough Orcières-Merlette ascent arrived. Ocaña climbed, unreachable in the summer light, almost unaware of the cheers of the crowd welcoming the arrival of a new icon. There would be an 8:42 wait for Merckx.

Ocaña took the yellow jersey that Merckx would soon attempt to get back by attacking on the road from Orcières to Marseille. Going all out, he would take only 1:56 off the yellow jersey after a 200 kilometer breakaway.

From now on, all eyes were fixed on the fourteenth stage, from Revel to Luchon, on July 11.

Ocaña knew the end of the stage very well, particularly the Col du Portillon. That is where he intended to attack and he didn't hide his intentions.

On the Col de Menté, a thunderstorm of unbelievable violence broke over the southern slopes of the pass. Visibility was reduced to 5 meters in all directions. "The Pyrenees

Ocaña personified simplicity, generosity, panache and this sport of cycling that he loved so much.

The two great protagonists of the 1973 Tour, Ocaña and Manuel Fuente, watch each other closely. Behind them, the ephemeral yellow jersey, Van Springel, lies in wait.

were prisoners of a somber wedding feast," wrote Paul Katz write in *Paris-Jour.* In a few seconds they were rubbing shoulders with the apocalypse.... Enormous hailstones crashed down on the race caravan, stinging and blinding the riders. The mountain rumbled and poured layers of silt onto the road.

Several miles further, a bend appeared. The riders sought their way through the mud. Suddenly, a cry came from the Bic team car: "Ocaña has crashed, right there in the middle of the bend!"

The yellow jersey was stretched out, covered in mud and in great pain. The preliminary examinations seemed reassuring. Ocaña had numerous contusions on his shoulders, head and torso, but no fracture was detected, simply a vertebral sprain.... He had felt himself invincible, responding to Merckx's attacks with unbelievable ease. Alas…

"I had advised Luis to let Merckx go," his directeur sportif, Maurice de Muer, told the press. He would have caught up with him later. But he preferred to give what he

had and meet him blow for blow. He was betrayed by his pride that day, his impetuousness." Merckx, now without a true rival, won the Tour for the third time running.

After health problems during the 1972 Tour, the Spaniard from Mont-de-Marsan returned to the 1973 Tour to win this time. There was no one to rival him, except perhaps his compatriot José Manuel Fuente.

Ocaña won the first stage, in the high mountains, between Divonne and Gaillard by way of Mount Salève, 6 miles from the finish. He distanced all his rivals, finding himself without any real opposition: Martinez, Fuente, Zoetemelk, Van Impe, Thévenet and Francisco Galdos were all left behind.

In the stage of the great passes—the Galibier and the Izoard—Fuente accompanied but did not help Ocaña. Soon he too had to drop back. Ocaña took the stage and reinforced his overall lead. He so greatly dominated this Tour, Pierre Chany wrote in *l'Equipe:* "It was a massacre, a general condemnation, a sort of collective annihilation."

Ocaña climbing the slopes of the Puy-de-Dôme, heading toward his fifth stage victory in this 1973 Tour, which he won without finding a single adversary to measure up to his talent.

Paths of Glory

Out of the trenches

In the 1922 Tour, Firmin Lambot (left) had the last word. Beside him stands his compatriot Hector Heusghem, who has just lost the yellow jersey, having received an hour's penalty for changing his bike.

Previous page: Roger Lapébie, capable of every exploit. Felice Gimondi, the astounding climber. Stephen Roche, a certain summer of '87. Marco Pantani, the mountain express.

Opposite: Léon Scieur, Honoré Barthélemy and Henri Colle, the revelation (walking his bike), in the last few hundred meters of the Galibier (Tour de France 1921).

Firmin Lambot (left), winner in 1922 as in 1919. The Belgian reign seemed to be becoming permanent. Next to him stands Joseph Pelletier, a good cyclist of the 1920s.

The 1919 Tour de France was monumental for several reasons. First of all, it commenced seven months after the armistice and many of its riders were World War I veterans. Henri Desgrange announced quite firmly that the Tour would be run under the twin signs of economy and austerity. "The cyclists," he declared, "should not imagine that we are going to feed them along the way."

The patron of the Tour also had to deal with some "strong heads," in particular Henri and Francis Pélissier.

Francis had a stroke of severe misfortune at the Paris start. The fork of his bike snapped clean through at the head tube. He could not change his bike—the rules were still draconian—and the rider had to go visit a mechanic on the Avenue de la Reine, in Boulogne-Billancourt, so that he could repair it himself. He worked for three hours, before cycling the 241 miles of the stage alone, arriving in Le Havre at night, just before the registration closed.

The war between Desgrange and the Pélissier brothers was far from over. After Henri won the second day in Cherbourg in front of his brother, Francis Pélissier showed his bad temper at the end of the fourth stage.

That reaction was no more than a fit of pique. Henri Pélissier let slip some unfortunately presumptuous remarks in Brest. "I am a thoroughbred," he claimed, "and my rivals are nothing but work horses."

This offended the whole of the peloton who thus decided to mount a fierce attack in the Côte de Quimperlé the following day. At the bottom of the town, Henri Pélissier stopped to take off his rain jacket. Was this yet another provocative gesture? At any rate, the riders took advantage of the situation and attacked explosively. In just a quarter of an hour Pélissier had lost the Tour, despite his 20-minute lead in the general classification. At the finish, a wildly resentful Pélissier directed a stream of invective at Desgrange who replied: "Henri's muscles are controlled by a poor little brain

Léon Scieur, winner of the 1921 Tour. A former agricultural laborer, he was a tireless and splendid fighter, nicknamed "the Locomotive."

which in just a few hours has tarnished a sporting reputation that could have been wonderful."

The Pélissiers quit the Tour, making way for a certain Eugène Christophe who, unluckily, as we have seen before, had to cede his yellow jersey to the Belgian Firmin Lambot.

The first-ever Tour winner in the history of the yellow jersey, Lambot did not cherish any real ambitions, preferring, in this Tour, to keep a quiet place at the front of the peloton. But circumstances would decide otherwise. He had a noted consistency. He finished the Tour eight times, winning it in 1922. A good road cyclist and a good climber, respectful of the regulations, always well equipped, rarely puncturing, the prudent rider from Florennes always had a certain sum of money on him so that he could buy a bike along the way, if he felt the need.

Léon Scieur and the invincible Belgians

Between the two victories of Firmin Lambot, the yellow jersey would remain in the hands of the Belgians. Apart from the victories of Philippe Thys and Scieur, Louis Mottiat, Félix Goethals, Jean Rossius, Emile Masson and Hector Heusghem each took their turn to wear the precious emblem.

Scieur was from Florennes, just like Lambot. The two men had a great and solid friendship and when they returned to their village in the Flemish Ardennes, near Namur, the beer flowed even more freely than usual. Scieur, a sturdy and hearty chap with a wide and welcoming smile, had only learned to ride a bike when he was twenty-two, just to be like… Firmin Lambot. In preparation for the 1921 Tour, Scieur, aged thirty-three, trained for three months but took part in only a few races: Paris-Roubaix, which he finished in third place, Paris-Dinant and the Belgian Championship.

From the first few stages, he resisted and responded to all of his rivals' offensives. In the 227-mile second stage, from Le Havre to Cherbourg, he dispossessed the excellent Mottiat of the yellow jersey. His physique was like a steel vault that enclosed a heart of gold. Add to that an iron will and relentless perseverance and you get a true road racer, who loved the road just as in the past he had loved the soil broken by the plough that he guided with his vigorous arms; indeed, Scieur was a loyal, generous and tenacious cyclist.

As soon as he took the leader's yellow jersey, one of the competitors, Honoré Barthélemy, cried out to the journalists: "When Scieur rides in his gear of 5.20 meters [equivalent to a gearing of 45 x 18], it's like having a locomotive in front of you! If he climbs the passes like he goes up the hills, where he's the one who sets the pace, then it remains to be seen if the so-called 'mountain men' will be able to keep up with him."

The verdict of Barthélemy—who was unfortunate enough in this Tour to beat the record for the greatest number of punctures—proved to be highly accurate. Nothing got the better of Scieur in this 1921 Tour. He climbed the mountains like the purest climber, rain or shine. No one could wrest the yellow jersey from him. His only direct rival in the Pyrenees was none other than his compatriot Hector Heusghem, who arrived alone in Luchon, with a 24-minute lead, lifting him into second place overall. He would attempt, with Barthélemy, to distance Scieur, in the Alps, when Scieur was obliged to stop to repair a puncture on the Col d'Allos. But a furious Scieur caught the two escapees and humiliated them by breaking away from them right under their noses. Heusghem didn't insist any further. Scieur would content himself to say rather prosaically: "I won the Tour de France because if you have the luck, at the start of the race, to see a bit of good fortune smile at you saying, 'If you are brave then I am yours,' that gives you a tremendous morale boost."

The science of Lucien Buysse

In 1926, the Buysse family won two out of the three yellow jerseys, with the third going to another Belgian, Gustave Van Slembrouck.

There were four Buysse brothers: the oldest, Marcel, was a very gifted cyclist, an unfortunate hero of the 1913 Tour, but too fond of life's pleasures. Lucien was another standout, and would win the Tour de France in 1926; then there was Cyril, who also had a talent for road racing. Finally there was Jules the youngest—twenty-five years old—who became the first yellow jersey of the 1926 Tour, after having led a beautifully stylish breakaway on the first stage to Mulhouse.

At the end of the third day, and its interminable 270-miles stage from Metz to Dunkirk, Van Slembrouck took over the yellow jersey. It was as if these Flemish gentlemen were amusing themselves by trading the colorful emblem like one might change shirts.

This Van Slembrouck was an astounding personality, holding onto the leader position until the Pyrenees. He shared his room with the excellent Omer Huyse, victor in 1924 of the longest Tour stage from Les Sables d'Olonne to Bayonne.

In Luchon, Huyse was awoken by a strange com-

Tenth stage of the 1926 Tour, from Bayonne to Luchon. The pivotal point of the race. In atrocious weather, through freezing fog and torrential rain, Lucien Buysse proved to be the best. He arrived in Luchon alone, winning the stage and taking the yellow jersey.

Lucien Buysse, father of four children, was thirty-four years old when he won the 1926 Tour. He invested his winnings in a café, which he named *l'Aubisque,* in memory of his exploit during the stage from Bayonne to Luchon.

Ottavio Bottecchia wins his second Tour de France in 1925. The "Mason of Friuli" would then leave the way open to his Belgian teammate, Buysse.

Maurice Dewaele: a shining example of perseverance rewarded (1929).

motion. He turned on the light and saw Van Slembrouck screaming and leaping around the room. Overcoming his fear he stopped his friend, shook him and urged him to calm down. But Van Slembrouck was having none of it: "You saw her just as I did, didn't you?" he asked breathlessly.

"But we're alone Gus, who do you mean?"

"The Holy Virgin! She was at the foot of my bed, all smiles, like she was mocking me. I pray to her every night and she made me lose my yellow jersey, the hussy! If I could've caught hold of her, I'd have strangled her, I'd have ripped her guts out!"

He eventually calmed down and went back to sleep. Huyse never sought further to discover the causes of this strange state of lunacy.

If Van Slembrouck's scepter had been withdrawn by the Virgin, then it was held firmly aloft by Lucien Buysse. Full of sturdy common sense, he had prepared his move very carefully, betting on the decline of his team leader and defending champion Ottavio Bottecchia.

The Tour had started badly for Buysse. The mud, the dust, the reflection of the sun on his glasses left him 10 minutes behind the leaders in Mulhouse, and half-blind. The treatment of an eye-specialist having improved both his sight and his confidence, Buysse bided his time. His chance came in the stage from Bayonne to Luchon, ten days later.

In the drizzle of the Col d'Aubisque, Buysse attacked, and passed the summit in the lead. Caught in the descent by Albert Dejonghe, he shook him off in the Tourmalet, but then Odile Tailleu surged past and crossed the summit in the lead. Bottecchia had long since quit the stage.

There still remained the Aspin and Peyresourde passes—which was where Buysse forged his success. The weather conditions had become impossible. A storm of unbelievable violence wiped out three-quarters of the peloton. Group by group, the riders collapsed under the torrential rain or in the icy fog of the passes. Buysse took advantage of the elements, catching and passing Tailleu. In the Aspin and Peyresourde passes, he revealed his true skill. His face relaxed, in spite of the mud, his eyes clear and lucid, as he rode at a steady pace in a harmonious pedaling rhythm. Buysse showed the power and ease on the climbs that made him the absolute victor of the 1926 Tour de France.

Buysse crossed the finish line in Luchon 25 minutes ahead of the runner-up Italian Bartolomeo Aimo. There was a three-quarter-of-an-hour wait for Léon Devos, Théophile Beeckman and Nicolas Frantz—that is, the phantoms who would complete the top-five finishers of this Dantesque stage. The Tour was already won for Buysse, of whom Karel Steyaert, editor of the Belgian paper *Sportwereld* and "pope" of Flemish cycling, would say: "Buysse is the cyclist who knows his Tour de France the best. He lives only for the Tour. He knows all of the roads and all of the pitfalls. He remembers all of the difficult bends; he has noted every bridge, every tree, every house and every point where he should turn a wheel round to shift gear. Lucien has the intelligence of the Tour de France."

Maurice Dewaele, from one leap to the next

"The 1929 Tour will be strictly and unquestionably individual." Henri Desgrange had set the tone. Taking into consideration the criticisms of the two previous Tours, he thus abandoned separate starts by teams, to return to the classic road-race format. The father of the Tour thus left it up to the cyclists themselves to take responsibility for and to fulfill their own demand that the sporting aspect of the race be maintained at all times, so as to avoid, in particular, the flat stages being run at a speed of 20 kph (12.2 mph). Suspicious by nature, Desgrange wrote in the regulations for the 1929 Tour: "Watch out, because the first time, except during the mountain stages, that you drop below 30 kph (18.3 mph), we will return to separate starts, until you have reached, in separate starts, a speed averaged in the corresponding stage of 1928..."

The Tour route hardly changed. However, to avoid an excessive distance, the Tour made its first foreign incursion, into Switzerland. From Evian it wended its way toward Geneva and left Switzerland by way of Ferney, picking up the old route again in Gex.

The favorite was Nicolas Frantz, winner of the two preceding Tours. Everyone was also expecting Victor Fontan, from the Béarn, to show his mettle

The first part of the race was clear and lively. After much scrambling the Tour reached Bordeaux, at the end of the seventh day, with three yellow jerseys: André Leducq and Frantz from the Alcyon team, and Fontan, who all shared the same time.

In the first mountain stage, from Bayonne to Luchon, Fontan and his friend Salvador Cardona gave it their all, with Cardona winning in Luchon and Fontan taking the yellow jersey.

But the euphoria in which the Basque and the Béarnais were swept up was short-lived. As the riders left Luchon, Fontan felt his frame give way beneath him, the fork broken. Fontan slumped as did his dreams.

Jef Demuysère proved to be the King of the Alps, but was unable to depose Maurice Dewaele, who won the 1929 Tour.

Share of the yellow jersey by country

FRANCE	78
BELGIUM	54
ITALY	23
NETHERLANDS	17
GERMANY	10
SPAIN & SWITZERLAND	7
LUXEMBOURG	6
DENMARK	5
GREAT BRITAIN	4
IRELAND	3
AUSTRALIA, CANADA & USA	2
AUSTRIA, ESTONIA, POLAND, PORTUGAL & RUSSIA	1

The first yellow jersey by country

FRANCE	Christophe (1919)
BELGIUM	Lambot (1919)
ITALY	Bottecchia (1923)
LUXEMBOURG	Frantz (1927)
AUSTRIA	Bulla (1931)
GERMANY	Stoepel (1932)
SWITZERLAND	Egli (1936)
NETHERLANDS	Van Est (1951)
SPAIN	Bahamontes (1959)
GREAT BRITAIN	Simpson (1962)
IRELAND	Elliott (1963)
AUSTRALIA	Anderson (1981)
DENMARK	Andersen (1983)
CANADA	Stieda (1986)
UNITED STATES	LeMond (1986)
POLAND	Piasecki (1987)
PORTUGAL	Da Silva (1989)
RUSSIA	Berzin (1996)
ESTONIA	Kirsipuu (1999)

Tour de France 1935. No one believed that Romain Maës could win it. Antonin Magne seemed to be the only real favorite.

The sturdy Maës won the 1935 Tour. He wore the yellow jersey from the first day to the last, and eliminated the favorites Magne and the Italian Francesco Camusso. He finally put an end to the French supremacy.

By a miracle, there was a spectator at the side of the road with a bicycle. He offered it to the Béarnais who set off, dazed, on the new bike, with the broken bike slung over his shoulder. He stopped at the first village he came to, less than 6 miles away. This time a garage owner agreed to help him out by giving him a suitable mount. It was not, alas, quite suited to the size of sturdy Victor. No matter, he adjusted a few parts to fit him better and set off again. But on the Col du Portet-d'Aspet he was already 36 minutes behind, with the arrival in Perpignan still more than 150 miles away. He would never be able to make it. A flood of tears overwhelmed him and he crashed again. He didn't finish the stage, beaten by this terrible misfortune. His yellow jersey went to the Belgian Maurice Dewaele.

In the Alps, another Belgian, Jef Demuysère, appeared to be the best, but he couldn't knock Dewaele off the leader position. And yet, at the start of the stage from Grenoble to Evian, Dewaele, with a corpselike pallor, fainted in the hotel toilets. His Alcyon teammates revived him and literally carried him to the start. They would continue to encourage him throughout the stage and enable him to reach Evian, more dead than alive.

He would keep his yellow jersey until Paris, but pay the price. "A corpse wearing a yellow jersey," said Henri Desgrange, who denounced the hegemony of the Alcyon team, affirming that the result did not conform to the sporting truth.

Romain Maës, the unexpected but absolute conqueror

Romain Maës was only twenty-two years old at the start of the 1935 Tour de France. But he won the first stage at Lille and so took the first yellow jersey.

"This yellow jersey," he cried, "on Romain's word, I'll keep it until Paris!"

His companions burst out laughing.

"Good old Romain! He's got a lot of guts for his age…."

And yet, he would keep his word.

A very good all-round cyclist, as incisive in a time-trial as he was in the mountains, he took all of the old hands by surprise, with his devilish lust to win. It was true that René Vietto was not quite himself this year, and that Antonin Magne dropped out after an accident, but all in all young Romain Maës didn't fear anyone and it's not certain that Magne could have beaten him, even on equal terms. He had great depth of character, with serious reserves of energy, courage in abundance and an extraordinarily fast capacity for recuperation. A mystery of athletic ability or a secret of muscular structure?

Nobody believed in the eventual victory of the little Belgian, since Magne took second place in the general classification at Belfort, the fourth stage finish. It was predicted that the French leader would assert himself even more in the Alps. But on the stage from Aix-les-Bains to Grenoble, Magne was struck by a car on the ascent of the Col du Télégraphe, and was forced to quit. This eliminated Maës's first major rival.

Two days later, the threat from Francesco Camusso of Italy was such that he was able to come within 3:31 of the leader. But Maës, who felt the danger, pushed himself to win in Cannes and so proved that he was clearly capable of winning the Tour de France. Then, on the flat stages before the Pyrenees, there was a veritable massacre of stars: Jules Merviel, Raffaele Di Paco, Roger Lapébie and…Camusso—who was taken out by another race vehicle.

So Maës saw his second big rival disappear; and then, on the final day, he treated himself to the great luxury of winning solo into the Parc des Princes, to the great joy of his mother who had left Belgium for the first time in her life so as to be able to embrace her son in all his glory.

Roger Lapébie, the fever and the fury

In the 1937 Tour de France, one name topped every list of predictions: Gino Bartali of Italy. Bartali confirmed his talent in the first few stages, but was knocked out of the running when he crashed in the Alps. After that, all eyes turned to Sylvère Maës, the defending champion from Belgium, who took the yellow jersey in Digne, at the end of the ninth stage. It looked as though he would win his second Tour victory, in spite of that stage's victory going to the Frenchman Roger Lapébie—who would soon move to second place in the general classification.

At the start of that year's Tour, Lapébie had quite a few doubts concerning his form. He wasn't sure if his back would hold out, having undergone an operation for a lumbar hernia after the Bordeaux-Paris classic. But he did have other things to cheer him up, like the use of a derailleur for the first time and a well known technical director, Jean Leulliot.

"For me," recounted Lapébie, "the Tour really started on the stage from Geneva to Aix-les-Bains. That particular day our French team lost Thiétard and Speicher. The next day, on the road to Grenoble, another blow struck us: Archambaud was hit by a car during the ascent of the Aravis.

Romain Maës greets his family, including his mother. who had left Belgium for the first time in order to witness his victory.

Maës does a lap of honor after winning the twenty-first and last stage, from Caen to Paris.

The 1937 Tour de France is won for Roger Lapébie.
It's time to celebrate with his fans and teammates.

After the Belgians withdrew in Bordeaux, with four stages
left to go, Roger Lapébie (center), technical director Jean
Leulliot (right), and teammate Paul Chocque (left) remain
concentrated but confident.

Then Le Grevès had to quit. We were down to six riders. At the hotel that evening, the boys said to me: 'The strongest guy is you. You're the only one that can win us some money.'" Lapébie thus set himself to winning the Digne stage. But although everyone spoke of the future victory of Maës, Lapébie saw the big favorite as the man who could lead him to victory. Henceforth he would stick to Maës like a shadow.

In Luchon, before attacking the Pyrenees, Lapebie had a good hunch about things, as the Belgian contingent in spite of their power had not been able to dominate him.

At the stage start in the spa town of Luchon, Lapébie waited for the Belgian attack. The peloton was gossiping and the word spread: we have to knock out Lapébie. That was when a little incident occurred, the details of which will never be known. But here is Lapébie's version: "Four minutes before signing the registration sheet, Jean Leuillot asked us to warm up. I set off, and the handlebars came away in my hands! Someone had removed them in order to saw through the bracket. Leuillot cried out that I'd had an accident. Quick, some handlebars! Everyone panicked. But they found some handlebars for me in a few moments, although without a water-bottle holder. The Belgians saw me trapped, and attacked right from the start. I immediately understood what had happened.

At the feed zone, no one was allowed to give me anything to drink. I had my fruit tarts, my rice cakes, my prunes and lots of sugar, but no water. The race-commissaires' car pulled in right behind me. I felt like I'd been set up. This sabotage destroyed me. At Garin, 3 miles after the start, I already felt shattered. I was drifting 5 minutes behind…"

In fact, at the summit of the first pass, the Peyresourde, Lapébie was only 2 minutes behind the yellow jersey, Maës. But nothing could hold back the Belgian team and their leader, while Lapébie, his forehead dripping with sweat, breathing deeply, his face lined with the strain and his eyes glazed, seemed crippled.

At the summit of the Col d'Aspin, the Frenchman was indeed almost 5 minutes behind. Discouraged, he talked of pulling out. Luckily for him, his teammate Paul Chocque turned out to be an extraordinary guardian angel, whose persuasion convinced him to continue.

On the Tourmalet, Lapébie picked up the pace. Ever the great fighter, he suddenly found some strength. He was told that up at the front Sylvère Maës had punctured. All of the Belgians were waiting for him and each of his teammates had to make a great effort to pace Maës up to the Spaniard Julian Berrendero, who had broken away on his own.

The effort caused the Belgians to fall apart shortly after the Tourmalet summit, which Lapébie passed 6:47 behind.

Maës really seemed to be exhausted, but he held on. Lapébie, informed of this, raced down the Tourmalet at such a speed that at the Argelès checkpoint he was only 3 minutes behind the leading group, composed of Maës, his teammate Felicien Vervaecke, another Belgian Edward Vissers, Berrendero and an Italian Mario Vicini. A bitter fight then ensued between the leaders and a chase group comprised of the Frenchmen Lapébie, Chocque, and Victor Cosson, Belgian Albertin Disseaux, Italian Francesco Camusso and the Dutchman Antoon Van Schendel.

In less than 9 miles, Maës had been caught. Seeing the powerful silhouette of the rival he thought he had crushed, appear at his side, the man in the yellow jersey could not help but have a look of resignation on his face. At the end of the stage, Berrendero and Vicini—who would puncture—succeeded in breaking away. The Spaniard won on his own and Lapébie, a minute back, took the seven-man sprint for second place. Lapébie was now just 1:33 behind the Belgian. What an exciting fight!

A fresh incident broke, when the inspectors awarded a penalty of 1:30 to Lapébie, because he had supposedly been given a push by some over-zealous spectators on the Col du Tourmalet.

There were more angry rumblings the next day in Bordeaux, the Frenchman's home turf, where the next stage would finish, a stage run in a most passionate atmosphere. During the race, Lapébie broke away from Maës, who the suffered a puncture that gave Lapébie the opportunity of his career. He seized it by shooting off like a rocket, taking 2:33 from his rival by the finish.

Then, right after the finish, the judges made it known that Maës, having received the illegal assistance of two Belgian cyclists not belonging to the national team, would be penalized 30 seconds. The Belgian kept the yellow jersey by just 35 seconds, three days from the end of the Tour.

That evening, in a dramatic turn of events, the penalty, considered unjustified by Maës, resulted in the withdrawal of the entire Belgian national team. From then on, the way was open for Lapébie, who took a sprint win in La Rochelle and led the French national team to victory in the team time trial at La Roche-sur-Yon. He won the Tour at an average speed of 19.716 mph, faster than Sylvère Maës the year before and a new Tour record.

Roger Lapébie benefited from a combination of favorable circumstances to win the 1937 Tour, but his talent was such that he could have done it all on his own.

A joyful meeting with the family after a victorious Tour de France for Lapébie.

Ferdi Kübler, the pedaling cowboy

Ferdi Kübler, the first-ever Swiss to win the Tour de France (1950).

Opposite: In the Alpine passes of the 1950 Tour, it was usually Kübler who took the initiative. Stuck right behind him, the Belgian Stan Ockers was never in a position to worry the Swiss.

Kübler resisted a Bobet "coup d'etat" on the stage from Briançon to Saint-Etienne in the 1950 Tour and regained the initiative. Behind him, Raphaël Géminiani gathers his strength before going on to win the stage.

The Swiss Ferdi Kübler only knew true fulfillment when he was attacking. He would stand up on the pedals and shout out before taking off. Nothing was too audacious for him. Fiery eyes, flared nostrils, he fidgeted on his bike like a man possessed. But what a rider!

Kübler wore the yellow jersey for the first time in the 1947 Tour de France, his first Tour, by winning the first stage. His success was short-lived in this Tour, though, since he alternated between good (in taking a second victory on the fifth stage) and bad (losing a half-hour on the third and sixth stage), before being eliminated, outside the time limit, on the eighth stage. But everyone knew he'd be back in the running since, in just a few days, he had given an indication of his potential.

He didn't start the 1948 Tour, didn't finish it the following year, then in 1950 he hit the bull's-eye and won the Tour. The task was not simple, though, for the young man from Zurich. His team was not as structured as the Italian or French teams. On the other hand, he decided to put an end to his headstrong ways and wild attacks. From now on he focussed entirely on following the tactics of the cunning and experienced Gino Bartali.

Kübler soon brought himself to everyone's attention by winning the sixth stage from Dinard to Saint-Brieuc, a time trial. But would the best time trialist be so comfortable in the mountains?

In Bordeaux, the day before the first Pyrenees stage, he was placed fifth in the general classification, ahead of all the pre-race favorites, including Bartali.

But a dramatic turn of events was about to unfold.

The best climbers started hostilities on the Col d'Aubisque, with Robic carving out a nice 3-minute lead over Bartali; but, victim of a fall, the Frenchman cracked on the slopes of the Tourmalet.

On the Col d'Aspin, Robic began to feel better and was soon riding alongside Louison Bobet, Stan Ockers and

On his return to the Tour in 1954, Kübler wanted to go even faster to beat Bobet. But Bobet's teammates, Raiyk Rémy (left) and Lucien Teisseire (right), put the brakes on.

Kübler won two stages at the 1954 Tour, but he never succeeded in winning the yellow jersey, and had to content himself with the green one (first on points).

Bartali. Suddenly, 200 meters from the summit, Bobet swerved and caused both Bartali and Robic to crash. The spectators rushed to help the men back into the saddle, but one of them had a knife in his hand and Bartali felt himself threatened, also claiming later that he had been punched. Extricated by some race followers, he set off again and won the stage in Saint-Gaudens. Kübler finished twelfth on the stage, almost 3 minutes behind.

That evening, in his hotel, Bartali announced that he was pulling out of the Tour, declaring: "I'm scared of the crazy people on the road; I've got a family and I mean to stay alive. I'm withdrawing."

His decision also resulted in the withdrawal of the entire national team, which included the new yellow jersey, Fiorenzo Magni.

Kübler would learn only the next day that he had become the race leader. But having considered the conditions in which the yellow jersey had landed on his shoulders, he refused to wear it at the start, and would only put it on that evening after the stage finish.

The Tour would really be played out on the next stage, a flat one, from Perpignan to Nîmes, in torrid heat. Kübler took off with Ockers and one of his Belgian teammates, and left Louison Bobet and his team 10 minutes behind.

From then on, the Swiss showed off with other lightning flashes, the most important of which came on the nineteenth stage between Briançon and Saint-Etienne.

Bobet, a magnificent fighter, thought that he could still win the Tour. He started the day in third place overall, 6:46 behind Kübler, and decided to surprise the Swiss by attacking him far from the finish. That was why at the Briançon start, where he had won the stage the day before, he sent off two of his teammates, Apo Lazarides and Pierre Molineris, who accompanied the regional rider Marcel Dussault. They would serve as hares and assist Bobet if he managed to outdistance the Swiss. At first, everything went according to plan.

Upon arriving in Grenoble, after 67 miles, and with 114 still to go, Bobet and teammate Géminiani shot straight through the feed zone, taking Kübler by surprise, and headed toward the Col du Saint-Nizier. Unfortunately, Géminiani soon sat up, and Bobet found himself pursuing his two hares on his own, riding like a maniac. He caught the 3 escapees, took 2 minutes off Kübler and had doubled his lead within another 12 miles. Ferdi was literally foaming with rage, sensing that victory was slipping from his grasp. He urged the Belgians Ockers and Raymond Impanis to help him. Ockers refused, since he was in second place overall. A single slipup by Kübler could put final victory in his lap.

Bobet found himself out on his own with Marcel Dussault, but the latter couldn't hold the pace and sat up. From here on the Frenchman was truly on his own. Behind him, the yellow jersey redoubled his efforts, since he had been told that the gap between himself and Bobet was quickly closing. His nose in the handlebars, deaf to the noise of the crowd and the cars, Kübler strained like a demon and soon had Bobet in his sights. But that was not enough. He decided to continue at the same pace and passed Bobet, shouting in triumph as he counterattacked. Louison had lost his last fight. Kübler took Tour victory, winning the final, 60-mile time trial, where he would beat Bobet by almost 10 minutes.

Kübler liked to have fun and was not without humor in his rather approximate French. One evening, at dinner, he was heard to protest loudly: "Chicken de Gaulle! Chicken de Goulle!" The hotel owner was ready to take offence until Ferdi clarified matters by pretending to stick his fork into the bird's carcass and saying: "Resistant! Resistant!" in reference to General de Gaulle's leadership of the French Resistance in World War II.

Kübler was meticulous in everything concerning his racing career. He would even call his coach in the middle of the night to notify him of a missing cleat on a shoe or of an improper crease in his cycling shorts. The night before an important stage, he demanded that no matter what, his bike should be taken up to his room before he went to sleep. In Briançon, the hotel owner did not agree and went off to complain to the Tour organizers. Useless to describe the burst of laughter that this solicited!

Roger Walkowiak, the "slandered" yellow jersey

Roger Walkowiak's story is a simple one, that of a man from the Marais quarter in Montluçon in the center of France, a young metalworker who became a Tour de France rider. Destiny crossed his path one day in the fine town of Angers, cool and calm, just like his personality. It was a beautiful afternoon in July 1956.

In his cycling career, Walkowiak had acquired the habit of taking, with apparent content, the places of honor: second in the Dauphiné Libéré, second in Paris-Nice and second in the Tour of the West—all week-long stage races.

At the start of the 1956 Tour de France, in Reims, he dreamed, not of winning the Tour, but of finishing best of the

Pulling on the yellow jersey, Roger Walkowiak suddenly realized the scope of a more brilliant destiny.

Roger Walkowiak in the 1956 Tour. Ever vigilant beneath his buttercup-colored jersey, he never thought he would attain such glory.

The yellow jersey covered "Walko" in glory. Trusty Walko, the metalworker turned Tour de France rider. (With his wife, Pierrette, and his team captain, Adolphe Deledda).

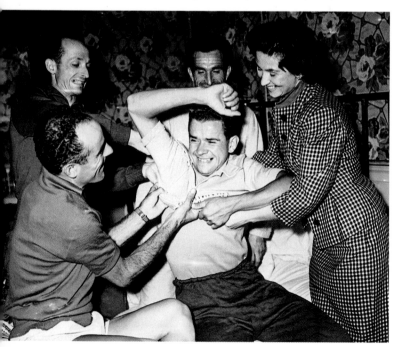

regional riders. He was a member of the Nord-Est-Centre team, managed by a certain Ducazeaux, whose first name promised much: Sauveur (Savior).

The Tour kicked off, with French national team sprinter André Darrigade taking the lead. But on the seventh stage, from Lorient to Angers, he lost the yellow jersey when 31 riders pulled away. There were many regional riders there, including Fernand Picot, Gilbert Scodeller and Nello Lauredi…a few Belgians, Italians and Dutch, but only one of Darrigade's teammates, Gilbert Bauvin. The breakaway increased in scope, and at the Angers finish, the stopwatches registered a time gap of 18:46.

The stage was won by the Italian Alessandro Fantini. But all eyes were focussed on the man who took the yellow jersey, the humble Walkowiak from Montluçon. That this supreme emblem should finally come to rest on "Walko's" shoulders was too much of an honor for him. He could hardly believe it, and burst into tears.

He finally accepted this gift of heaven and managed, once alone in his room, to look himself in the mirror. After all, it suited him just as well as the other riders. He promised himself that evening, to defend the jersey for a few days, until one of the "greats," destined for final victory, came to take it away from him. He could never have imagined what was to happen to him….

Despite his growing portliness, team director Ducazeaux shot up the stairs two at a time to the new Tour leader's room. Even before congratulating him, he told Walkowiak straight out: "Roger, I think that you can win the Tour de France!"

"Walko" thought for a moment that his manager was teasing him. He was not a man to laugh at a friend though, and yet how could he say such a thing? He was neither a genius nor a poseur; he was just humble "Walko" from Montluçon whose merits were vaunted only by the local papers.

He might be pardoned for not having listened to Ducazeaux very much that particular evening. His thoughts lay with his young wife, Pierrette, whom he had married the previous Christmas. While the Nativity had marked the wedding of this junior secretary at the Department of Mines and this ex-metalworker, they had to wait for their true gift. It came in the form of the yellow jersey, in good quality wool, which represented perhaps the first foundation stone of a home that would shelter their happiness.

At dinner, Ducazeaux was categorical and surprising: "Roger. You have to lose this yellow jersey…in order to take it back later." So Roger, as instructed, lost it three days later when seventeen riders—including Darrigade and Bauvin—gained 14 minutes on the flat roads to Bayonne.

The Tour then "drank" a little Garonne, jumped over the Pyrenees, cruised through the vineyards of Hérault and Provence, and slid, intoxicatingly, up to the Alps. The leader was now Dutchman Wout, who was still in yellow starting the eighteenth stage from Turin to Grenoble, with Walkowiak in second, 4:27 back. Ducazeaux had chosen to mount his attack here, in the Vercors range, a hotspot of the French Resistance in World War II.

And Walkowiak, devilishly aggressive, managed to stick with the top climbers like Bahamontes, and took back the yellow jersey in Grenoble, now 3:56 ahead of the persistent Bauvin. Walko then defended his lead in the final time trial, despite conceding 2 mintues to Bauvin.

Like a tempestuous whirlwind, this time, all the honors fell to Little Walkowiak. At the Parc des Princes, when he dared to look around him, they were already awarding him the final day's yellow jersey, that of the coronation, the lap of honor. Roger looked tenderly at his wife and then, shyer, more moved and more overwhelmed than her, let a tear slip onto his golden mantle.

But already certain members of the press and a certain ruling class had started to contest his success: Walko had won his Tour on the flat and so was not a true champion, the said. Nothing could be more false. He alone knew the price paid for such a victory. And yet the name of Walkowiak, the "slandered" yellow jersey, would not get more than a single line in the annals of cycling. But that at least can never be taken away from him.

Raphaël Géminiani, "the Long Rifle"

He had class to spare and a wonderful personality. With his colorful ways, he was fully qualified to become a cycling legend. Raphaël Géminiani was one of the rare French cyclists to have shared the privilege of wearing the leader's jersey at the Tours of France, Italy and Spain.

The "Long Rifle," as Louison Bobet nicknamed him one evening after a stage at the 1955 Tour de France, spent 17 years of his life on a bike and took part in 12 Tours de France, winning 7 stages.

He was also one of the first to anticipate the evolution of cycling. An innovator, he brought a non-cycling sponsor into the peloton, by associating his name with a brand of aperitif that bore his name. The accession of the Géminiani-

Fifth stage of the 1958 Tour de France. The French team shot straight through the feed zone at Orbec-en-Auge and broke away. The attack was launched by Anquetil, Bobet and Bauvin, with Bauvin taking the yellow jersey at the stage finish in Caen. But Géminiani (behind Bauvin) made a big leap on general classification.

The regional rider Géminiani has just taken the yellow jersey, thereby snubbing the French national team. A group of his fellow Auvergne musicians insist on paying homage to him, with hurdy-gurdy and accordion (1958 Tour).

Géminiani tried everything
against Hugo Koblet,
the yellow jersey, but in vain
(1951 Tour, Mont Ventoux).

The "greats" allowed themselves to relax a
little during the last stage of the 1951 Tour.
From left to right: Géminiani, Bobet, Koblet
(yellow jersey) and Coppi.

Saint-Raphaël team was the fruit of one of the smartest intuitions that cycling has seen.

As for his racing career, he spent years in the trenches—his first selection for the Tour de France was in 1947—before earning his first yellow jersey in 1958. Géminiani was then thirty-three years old.

That particular year, at the start of the race in Brussels, he was still brooding over his omission from the French team. It would never be known who was at the origin of this eviction, but the rumor ran that it was Anquetil, who asked technical director Marcel Bidot to avoid a Bobet-Géminiani collusion at any price.

From then on, Géminiani, who took a place in the Centre-Midi team, openly declaring himself the leader of the opposition. He sniffed out all attacks, slipped into the most paying breakaways, and shouted down Bidot's men, refusing to cooperate with them during the breakaways. Upon leaving Brittany, after the first seven stages, Géminiani placed third overall. Never had he been so confident in the way things were going.

On the national team, Bobet confided in a few journalists: "The tough guy in the mountains will be Raphaël. He has never been so strong. He has never ridden so well; he is always at the front. This time, he has the mindset of a winner, like Gaul. And he is supported by eleven guys with nerves of steel. He has galvanized them."

Then came the mountains and thirteenth stage, from Dax to Pau. The "Long Rifle" was ready to fire.

His big target was the Aubisque. On reaching the day's main climb, the morning's breakaways had been caught and passed by Bahamontes. Behind, came the stars of the Tour including the usual suspects, Gaul and Géminiani. Soon, the man from Luxembourg accelerated and headed off alone. "Gem" let him go. He knew that Gaul would be caught on the flat run-in to Pau—where he, Géminiani, would realize the dream, that he had spent 9 Tours racing after the yellow jersey.

The great event had finally arrived, with Géminiani taking winning his yellow jersey by just 3 seconds over the Italian, Vito Favero.

"Got it," he cried. "Now you'll have to chase me for it!"

"He had a stupendous morale," remembers his directeur sportif, Adolphe Deledda, "but he was very excited and, from then on, he became more and more anxious. He was no longer the spontaneously jovial Géminiani I had always known. He would have to go against his nature to win the Tour. Until then, he had tended to believe in it as a tactic and to impress his adversaries. This time it was the real thing. That evening we drank a bottle of champagne. We knew that it would be tough to win but we were confident."

The next day, the Long Rifle would cede his yellow jersey to Favero, but Géminiani would take it back on the Mont Ventoux stage, a time trial, which was won by Charly Gaul.

In the stage from Gap to Briançon, over the Vars and Izoard passes, he kept his cool. Gaul was more than 16 minutes behind him on the general classification and Anquetil 7:52. The following stage, from Briançon to Aix-les-Bains, through the Chartreuse mountains, was going to be formidable, due not only to the terrain, but also the atrocious weather conditions.

Géminiani fought valiantly all day and countered all those who plotted his downfall. Alas, he ended up defeated, completely worn out, in spite of the support from his loyal Centre-Midi teammates. It was as if fate had united with his rivals against him, in the form of a broken toe-clip, which forced him to stop on the Col de Porte. It was a pitiful sight seeing Gem burst into tears, worn out, bemoaning his misfortune and calling the French team "Judases."

He was 15 minutes behind Charly Gaul at the finish, the absolute victor in the deluge, and more than 4 minutes behind Favero. The yellow jersey, that he had won with such panache and defended with such ardor, and that he had dreamed of wearing at the Parc des Princes, had been snatched from him by the Italian Favero for a second time. He would soon cede it definitively to Gaul. "I live only for this marvelous adventure," Géminiani had said so many times, and now he had lost it just when he had a glimpse of a happy conclusion.

Raphaël Géminiani, the fighter, the number one aggressor, deserved every praise.

Gastone Nencini or the danger averted

At the start of the 1960 Tour de France, the French national team was the strong favorite, led by its figurehead Roger Rivière, the world hour record holder and invincible in time trials. A significant indication of his strength was given by Jacques Anquetil, that year's winner of the Tour of Italy, who declined the invitation to take part in the Tour, not wishing to be compared with this rising star who might have snatched his popularity from him.

From the start, the Italian star, Gastone Nencini, gained the most from a first half-stage run at a crazy speed

DE GAULLE AND THE TOUR DE FRANCE

On July 16, 1960, the Tour's twentieth stage from Besançon to Troyes passed through Colombey-les-Deux-Eglises. The race director decided to stop the peloton to salute the President of the Republic who had come from his nearby home with his wife to watch the Tour pass. "A respectful silence," wrote the journalist André Herné in the Télégramme de Brest. "I never thought that someone could actually halt the hullabaloo of the Tour." In front of General de Gaulle is the yellow jersey Nencini with, on his left, Antonin Rolland, doyen of the peloton, and, on his right, Jean Graczyk, the green jersey.

Every year, Gastone Nencini
found a way of asserting
himself in the Tour. In 1956
it was a stage victory, and,
in 1957, the King of the
Mountains title (here seen
leading the Belgian Janssens).

Nencini didn't see the Tour as an epic challenge.
Rather he tried, every day, to be true to himself
and worthy of his tough profession.

and won by the Belgian Julien Schepens. And that evening, in Brussels, following a short second half-stage time trial won by Rivière, Nencini took the yellow jersey. He certainly didn't expect to keep this "jacket" for long. When you race to win an event such as the Grande Boucle, you shouldn't have to do too much work—which was why the yellow jersey passed to the Breton sprinter Joseph Goussard on the third day in Dieppe, following a stage won by the Italian Nino Defilippis. Then the French team went into action and Henry Anglade took the overall lead for two days before the coup d'état on the sixth stage from Saint-Malo to Lorient.

A real thunderbolt!

Nencini broke away, taking with him the Belgian Jean Adriaennseno, the German Hans Junkermann and Rivière. The quartet stuck together, never ceasing to increase their lead, and reached Lorient at an average speed of 27.353 mph, with Rivière beating Nencini in the sprint. The four men had carved out a quarter of an hour lead for themselves over the rest of the riders!

One can understand Anglade's anger, his jersey taken by one of his own. But above all, everyone noted the size of the lead.

In the general classification, the yellow jersey now went to Adriaennseno, with Nencini in second place, Rivière third and Junkermann fourth. Given the quality of these four men, one might well have predicted that one of them would be the final victor.

And thus the Tour bore a sense of finality for much of the time.

On the tenth day, in Pau, Rivière won another stage, but Nencini took the yellow jersey, 32 seconds ahead of Rivière. That day, climbing the Col d'Aubisque, the Italian and his compatriot Graziano Battistini rudely tested the Frenchman's inexperience. But Rivière caught them up on the descent, and had the panache to beat them in the sprint for stage victory.

Now, all that anyone spoke of was the Nencini-Rivière duel.

What would the mountain stage from Pau to Luchon bring? Rivière made the mistake of not protecting himself sufficiently against the cold when starting the descent of the Tourmalet to Sainte-Marie-de-Campan. Things brightened for him later, but Nencini felt himself to be the master of the situation. He attacked on the Col de Peyresourde and Rivière could do nothing but look on, powerless. The Italian ate up the slope and managed to take another 66 seconds from Rivière, while the stage was won solo by the Swiss Kurt Gimmi.

With Nencini in complete control, what else did Rivière have up his sleeve to outdistance him? It was a tricky situation, since he couldn't rely on distancing Nencini on the descents—which were the Italian's favorite terrain. Hadn't Bobet reminded Rivière of what Anquetil had told him after the Tour of Italy?

The triple winner of the Tour told him: "Roger, don't forget that if you want to chase Nencini in the descents then you have to want to die."

Roger must have neglected to take sufficient care, for in the Cevennes, during the stage from Millau to Avignon, the world record holder attempted to outdistance the yellow jersey in the descent of the little Col du Perjuret, on the slopes of the Aigoual Mountain. But Rivière was no match for Nencini at this game, and crashed into a ravine. He would never ride a bike again.

From then on, Nencini was without a rival. The Tour had thus truly been won in Lorient, at the end of that sixth stage, as had been felt at the time.

That year, the Tour made a once-in-a-century stop in the village of Colombey-les-Deux-Eglises, on the stage from Besançon to Troyes. General de Gaulle had insisted on coming to applaud the riders from his nearby home, saluting first the yellow jersey and then the front-line riders such as Darrigade, Anglade and Antonin Rolland.

At the Paris finish, in the Parc des Princes, Nencini gave his winner's wreath to Marcel Bidot, technical director of the French team, for him to give to the unfortunate Rivière. Nencini won everyone's heart by this action.

With the looks of a Sioux chief, his small slanting eyes and craggy face masked a hypersensitive individual. He was interested in French second-class riders and got on well with these men, who were quite removed from the leading lights of the peloton. He was never without a little cigarette—he particularly liked Gauloises—and drank a few glasses of fine red wine with his meals. Quite simply, Nencini loved life.

In the Pyrenees, during the 1960 Tour, Nencini bent the Frenchman Roger Rivière to his will. An excellent climber, he was also the best descender in the peloton, something that Rivière would discover to his cost.

Nencini was nicknamed the "Lion of Tuscany." A top quality cyclist on any terrain, he made his Tour de France debut in 1960 with a previous Tour of Italy victory.

Felice Gimondi, the long career of a gentleman

The podium of the 1965 Tour: Felice Gimondi (first), Raymond Poulidor (second) and Gianni Motta (third).

In the 1965 Tour, the Italians to watch went by the names of Vittorio Adorni and Motta, but Gimondi would prove himself an opportunist, revealing ambitions that had been hidden until then.

A star is born: Felice Gimondi (center), a young stallion of twenty-three selected for the 1965 Tour against his will, very soon joined the Tour's cast of "superstars."

dolized and revered, Felice Gimondi was the subject of a true cult for Italy's passionate fans. Winner of the 1964 Tour de l'Avenir amateur race, the young champion made a sensational entry the following year into the professional ranks by winning the Tour de France at just twenty-three years of age, beating Poulidor and Gianni Motta in the process.

Events took an unexpected turn that year. The young man from Bergamo had just turned professional by joining the Salvarani team, led by Vittorio Adorni. He immediately finished third in the Tour of Italy, an excellent result for a neo-professional, attaining the goal fixed for him by his directeur sportif, the wise Luciano Pezzi. But since it was only his first year as a professional, there was no question of him lining up for the Tour de France. Events would decide otherwise.

When it came to selecting his team for the Tour de France, Pezzi had a little difficulty. Several of his choices were sick. The team director could see only one solution… Gimondi.

The young professional didn't understand it. Hadn't the very same man advised him not to participate in two big Tours the same year? And now…

The president of Gimondi's cycling club and his deputy were clearly against the selection, but Pezzi insisted. Gimondi asked himself: "Suppose I start the Tour de France but then have to withdraw. Who'll want anything to do with me after that? My career will be finished." Pezzi replied: "Well then, sign the contract for next year. But look out! Since I'm sure that you'll do well in this Tour de France, you'll be worth more then. But it'll be too late and you'll already have signed."

But Gimondi insisted and the 4-million lire contract for 1966 was drawn up and signed straight away.

After that, everything happened as in a dream. From the second day, in Roubaix, he was already in second place overall, behind the Belgian Bernard Vandekerkhove. The third day, in Rouen, he won the stage and took the yellow jersey.

One could hardly imagine a better start to things. The test of the cobblestones, a nightmare for non-Flemish Tour novices, didn't give him any problems at all, although one should remember a little detail: at the start of the season, Gimondi took part in the Paris-Roubaix race finishing incognito, but he had carefully noted down his observations in an exercise book, to which he referred to in the Tour to refresh his memory.

But what had become of Poulidor, the great favorite of this Tour in the absence of Jacques Anquetil? The Frenchman won the time trial in Châteaulin, on the fifth day, but Gimondi lost only 7 seconds.

Then, on the seventh stage from La Baule to La Rochelle, Vandekerkhove took his yellow jersey back, but it seemed pretty clear that it would only be temporary. The big Belgian was no climber, and a few days later in the stage mountain from Dax to Bagnères-de-Bigorre, fought out under a fierce heatwave, Vandekerkhove had to quit. Also KO'd were Adorni—Gimondi's team leader—and Lucien Aimar, Hans Junkermann and Rolf Wolfshohl. The Spaniard Julio Jimenez won the stage and Gimondi took the yellow jersey back. Would Poulidor finally react? Mont Ventoux served his purpose. Poupou won the stage, and moved to within 34 seconds of Gimondi overall. Everyone expected an upset in the Alps, particularly on the Mont Revard, a 17-mile uphill time trial. But Gimondi surprised everyone again, taking a 23-second victory over Poulidor and then winning the last stage, also a time trial, between Versailles and Paris.

As the new leader of Italian cycling, Gimondi would never win the yellow jersey again but always proved to be competitive, building one of the most admirable career records in cycling history. In particular, he won the Tour of Italy, the world championship, Milan-San-Remo, Paris-Roubaix, Paris-Brussels, the Tour of Spain, Tour of Lombardy and Grand Prix des Nations.

Lucien Aimar, his master's voice

In 1966, the Anquetil-Poulidor rivalry reached its peak and divided France into two rival clans when Anquetil won Paris-Nice in the last stage, and Poulidor then accused him of colluding with other teams.

The Tour de France would thus kick off under the sign of this incessant struggle between the two individuals. Poulidor hardly hid his ambition of wanting to win the Tour. As for Anquetil, he had already won the Tour 5 times, but accepted to take part in the race upon the request of his di-

Lucien Aimar would never forget July 14, 1966.

Last lap of the 1966 Tour for Aimar on the last stage, a time trial, from Rambouillet to Paris.

Aimar managed to outwit Poulidor's vigilance. He broke away on the road to Turin, the seventeenth stage finish, and took the yellow jersey.

recteur sportif Raphaël Géminiani as the road captain of the Ford-France team. In fact, Anquetil didn't show the slightest desire to race for the victory. If he started at all, then it was surely to prevent his rival Poulidor from winning, and also to help one of his own teammates win, perhaps Lucien Aimar, who promised great things. After all, he had been one of the best amateur racers, before turning professional under the firm rule of the skillful Géminiani.

Cunning and intelligent, knowing how to make the most of his physical abilities, Aimar was very guarded concerning his intentions. He would wait for the right moment to present itself, but he first of all put himself at the service of his team leader, Anquetil.

For Aimar, the adventure started rather discreetly in the Pyrenees. But his efforts would have major consequences later on. Everyone expected some skirmishes between Poulidor and Anquetil on the road from Bayonne to Pau. In the end, the stage turned out to be a total confusion for the two favorites.

A young Lombard, a teammate of long-time race leader Rudi Altig, Tomasso de Pra, won the stage and took the yellow jersey. And the others? Twenty riders took off and quickly formed a lead group, in which one searched in vain for Anquetil and Poulidor. On the other hand, two dark horses were in this group: Dutchman Jan Janssen and Aimar. Also in front were other potentially dangerous men—like Raymond Delisle, Jos Huysmans, Jean-Claude Lebaube, Guido De Rosso and Valentin Uriona—who crossed the finish line more than 7 minutes ahead of the peloton. Janssen, in second overall, was now the big threat but Aimar's potential was also apparent.

Of course the press was plunged into endless questionings about the attitude of the two divas, Anquetil and Poulidor. How could they have let such a situation develop? Anquetil pointed out that since Aimar was up front, he was obliged to play the role of a supporting team member. Poulidor could not oppose such an argument, thus irritating his directeur sportif, Antonin Magne, who declared: "Decidedly, I'll never be able to understand Poulidor!"

The evidence was all too clear: except for a major upset in the situation, the two great favorites of the Tour were already beaten.

They were both conscious of this. The next day, during the stage from Pau to Luchon, the two men recognized and discussed their guilty passivity and decided to act.

A serious clean-up operation ensued. The Spaniards Joaquim Galera, Jimenez and Gregoria San Miguel, as well as

The élite of the 1966 Tour. Aimar wears the yellow jersey, with Pingeon (right) and Poulidor (left).

Roger Pingeon and Delisle, made a strong attack on the Col de Menté. The inseparable Anquetil-Poulidor duo responded with astounding vigor. Suddenly, half the peloton fell back between the Menté and Portillon passes. Mugnaini, Kunde and Lebaube, who one didn't expect in the front, asserted themselves. Janssen and Aimar also answered the call and all eyes were now focused on them.

Poulidor had pulled himself together by now, but was it too late? In the time trial at Vals-les-Bains, he beat Anquetil by 7 seconds, after having made a true demonstration of power. A glance at the rankings showed that Aimar had finished only 47 seconds back and Janssen 57 seconds.

But Poulidor continued to believe. Between Privas and Bourg-d'Oisans, he attacked on a slippery descent in driving rain and crossed the line a minute ahead of Anquetil. One sensed a certain lassitude in the 5-time winner's bearing. He no longer burned with zeal. The risk-taking was over.

He did not wish, however, to captiulate to Poulidor and, in the following stage, from Bourg-d'Oisans to Briançon, won by the Spanish climber Julio Jimenez, Anquetil took second place, in front of Poulidor. But neither one nor the other could close the gap created in the Pyrenees and, that evening in Briançon, Janssen took the yellow jersey.

Everything hinged on the seventeenth stage the following day, from Briançon to Turin. Eight riders attacked on the Col de Coletta, among them Franco Bitossi, Herman Van Springel and Wolfshohl. As the grade steepened, the peloton split into several groups. Poulidor then accelerated and broke away on his own.

Behind, sensing danger, the other race leaders reacted. Aimar and Janssen were riding wheel to wheel. Aimar gave Anquetil a questioning look and received his support. Even better, the Norman deliberately went to the front and stretched out the group. In about 1½ miles Poulidor was in

As discreet in glory as he was generous in effort: Aimar with Janssen (second, on right) and Poulidor (third).

Poulidor paces Pingeon up the Galibier, pursuing Gimondi, who had broken away on the stage to Briançon. In a French team with diverse interests, Poulidor accentuated his "Poupoularity" and Pingeon acquired the limelight that he deserved.

sight. This was the moment to take advantage of the pause which nearly always comes after a rider is caught. Anquetil suggested to Aimar that he attack.

The rider from the Côte d'Azur threw himself into the task. Poulidor and Janssen didn't respond. Aimar joined the group of 8 men and by the finish had gained more than 2 minutes on his challengers, taking the yellow jersey.

Once again Poulidor was trapped. Despite his lightning attack on the following stage from Ivrea to Chamonix, where he climbed the Forclaz in an extraordinary show of force, he was able to take only 49 seconds off Aimar. The next day, Anquetil, suffering from the beginnings of a congestion of the lungs, withdrew from the Tour on the Côte de Serrières. His task, with regard to Aimar, was accomplished. Determined and driven, Aimar was able to stave off the remaining attacks by Janssen, who was able to make up only 28 seconds of his 1:35 deficit in the last day's individual time trial.

The great talent of Roger Pingeon

For the analysts, it is clear that Roger Pingeon was a very special case in the annals of cycling.

It should be noted, first of all, that he had such an enormous talent that his morale had trouble keeping up with it. At the slightest unusual sensation in his long body, all of his senses went on high alert. He mistrusted everything and gave the impression that at any minute the sky would fall on his head or, according to the words of Roger Bastide, both of his tires would burst at the same time or his derailleur would fall into his spokes.

In 1967, the Tour de France returned to the formula of national teams. On the French team, Poulidor and Aimar joined forces with Roger Pingeon.

Pingeon! No one in the peloton doubted his capacities, and certainly not the French technical director Marcel Bidot. From the Angers start, Jean Stablinski, road captain of the French team, said to him: "You're just tickling the pedals, Roger. Take advantage [of your good form], go up front, try something."

He finally did as suggested during the fifth stage, from Roubaix to Jambes. Again it was due to the intervention of the very same Stablinski, who saw that a breakaway was forming ahead, including Rik Van Looy, Vandekerkhove, Desiré Letort, Jean-Claude Theillière, Guy Ignolin and Raymond Riotte. A dozen men in all. So heeding "Stab," Pingeon shot out of the peloton and there he was, heading off, like one might go to mass. Those following admired the harmonious style of his long limbs, as he attacked the roads of Hainaut and Namur, sprinkled with their treacherously steep hills.

He caught the breakaways, apparently without any problem. His teammate Riotte didn't seem a bit surprised, and he as the one who encouraged Pingeon to redouble his efforts.

They came to the Mur de Thuin, a steep, cobbled climb. Pingeon accelerated. His companions dropped back one by one, and the rider from Bugey headed off on a solo break of 37 miles. At the finish, where his teammate Riotte took second place, Pingeon had shocked all of the race favorites by taking more than 6 minutes off them. A wonderful exploit worthy of a yellow jersey winner.

Even though he lost it for one day in Strasbourg, to the courageous Riotte, Pingeon recaptured the lead the next day at the Ballon d'Alsace finish. On this long day in the Vosges mountains, Poulidor was plagued by crashes and mechanical problems, and ended the stage 10 minutes behind the leaders, totally exhausted. Pingeon himself almost went the same way, but was saved by a slice of gingerbread spontaneously and generously given to him by the Italian Felice Gimondi. Pingeon found all his strength again and the yellow jersey, at the finish of the stage which was won by Aimar.

From then on Poulidor put himself at his teammates service, so that he could better handle the attacks from Jimenez and Gimondi in the mountains. But he was able to assert his style, a style which suited him well, since Pingeon would remain a one-off. He refused to ride to his hotel, considering it pointless to add to the day's fatigue. His room number was kept a secret so that he would not be disturbed, and he gave interviews in the bathtub, because every minute counted. He insisted on being the first on the massage table and turned up late for dinner, so as not to have to put up with slow service.

"I don't do an ordinary job," he confided, "so I don't try to live like an ordinary person."

Pingeon took care every night to study the route of the next stage and check the weather. Before going to sleep, he blocked off any source of light in his room, going so far as to stuff the keyholes with cotton wool, and put a bandana over his eyes.

The night before a rest day, he took an evening meal without any sugars or carbohydrates in it. The next day, when his comrades would leave the hotel to ride for miles, Pingeon opted for absolute rest and stayed stretched out on his bed practically all day. He cut out sugars in all of his

Pingeon and the French team. On left, from top: Poulidor, Stablinski, Novak, Riotte and Genet. On right, from top: Jourden, Guyot, Samyn and Raymond.

Pingeon, yellow jersey, with Genet (left) and Riotte. The French team radiated a feeling of real harmony.

Jan Janssen, the hard-hitter from the Netherlands, knew how to motivate himself at the key moments.

Janssen, the first Dutch winner of the Tour (1968).

meals that day, as well as meat, eating simply raw vegetables, fish and fruit.

He had another light meal in the evening and afterwards, to crown it all, took a hot bath into which he dissolved 5 pounds of salt and a few liters of wine vinegar. It was a kind of light sauna, lasting generally less than 10 minutes, whose sweating effects were guaranteed and which served above all as a pick-me-up, due to the mixture of salt and vinegar.

Having thus eliminated all toxins, Pingeon, a guy unlike the others, was one of the first attackers the following day.

What was lacking? With a bit more confidence he would have been capable of anything.

Jan Janssen, the first Dutchman to win the Tour

When Jan Janssen—born May 19, 1940—became world champion in 1964 at Sallanches, France, beating Adorni and Poulidor, it was clear that a great career had commenced. In just two years of professional cycling he had become one of the top stars. Cycling, for which he had sacrificed his adolescent passion for speed skating, was well-suited to his talents: an attacker's temperament, but above all a certain class.

He got his first bike when he was fifteen, as a reward for a brilliant performance in his school exams, which enabled him to go to the technical high school of the Hague. Three years later, he started competitive cycling.

A strong rider on the flat and a great sprinter, the Dutchman knew how to take pain. He would even develop impressive climbing skills in the high mountains, where he astounded his rivals by his consistency. He could have won the Tour de France in 1966, if a certain Lucien Aimar hadn't got in his way. Janssen had taken the yellow jersey in Briançon, leading Aimar by 27 seconds. The peloton bristled with such formidable names as Jacques Anquetil, Raymond Poulidor, Roger Pingeon and Julio Jimenez. But Janssen had proven his great determination that day, in deciding to dispossess the German Karl-Heinz Kunde of his yellow jersey. The stage crossed the Col du Galibier and one might have thought that Janssen, by taking over the reins of the Tour on such a selective stage, had given himself every chance of winning the Tour.

The profile of the following days' mountain stage was only a medium one, a walk in the park for Janssen, especially since the stage was followed by a rest day.

But that particular day, who knows why, the Dutchman let his guard slip and, in the Col de Coletta, Aimar decided to chase the eight riders who were 2:30 ahead. Thanks to a wonderful effort, Aimar managed to catch up with some of the breakaways and finished the day 2 minutes ahead of Janssen.

"I didn't see him," Jan Janssen still admits today. "When he attacked on a narrow winding road, I was in the second half of the peloton. It was my compatriot Henk Nijdam who warned me. 'Hey, Jan, Aimar has broken away!' At first, I didn't believe it, but after looking for him I realized that he had indeed gone."

His directeur sportif had not told Janssen, since the Tour radio had broken down at the moment of the attack and the race followers knew nothing of the situation.

Janssen's turn to win the Tour de France came two years later, and it came at the eleventh hour—on the final stage, a time trial, between Melun and Paris.

Going into the time trial, the top nine riders were separated by only 2:30. Such was the extraordinary suspense of the most unusual Tour de France of the post-war period.

"That morning," remembers Janssen, "I was third in the general classification, 16 seconds behind the Belgian Van Springel. We had raced a first half-stage that morning, where I hadn't had to make much effort. But we had to remain vigilant, since my team was down to just Beugels, Den Hertog, Dolman and myself. Everything hinged on that afternoon. I was certainly ready, but had never raced such a long time trial before (47 miles). The favorite was Van Springel, who was a time trial specialist. But I wanted to give my all.

"After 2 miles I already had a 15-second lead over the Belgian and I heard the crowd screaming 'Janssen the winner' or 'Janssen, you've got the jersey.' To hear those kind of things motivates you more than anything. I understood that I was in the process of winning the Tour de France. When I saw Van Springel arrive at the 'Cipale track, he seemed to have lost his grip. I knew then that I had won."

Janssen thus brought the Dutch their first Tour victory, crowning one of the most beautiful career records in cycling, which included, in particular, victories in Paris-Roubaix, Bordeaux-Paris, the Tour of Spain, Paris-Nice and, of course, the world championship.

The time of reckoning approaches for Jan Janssen. He had known so much disappointment and doubt in the Tour de France. Could he be the man of the moment in 1968?

Whether belonging to the Bic, Pelforth or Mercier teams, they all had the same ambition: the yellow jersey. Only one of them would never win it. From left to right: Anquetil, Janssen and Poulidor.

The unexpected success of Joop Zoetemelk

The 1973 Tour. Joop Zoetemelk, a prophet in his own country, has just won the prologue in Scheveningen, becoming the first yellow jersey of the race.

Joop Zoetemelk won the Grande Boucle in his tenth participation.

C hampions who have worn the yellow jersey many times will all tell you that the first time they put it on was the best.

For Joop Zoetemelk, the great moment took place on July 7, 1971. The stage finished in Grenoble. The Tour was heating up, and Eddy Merckx was starting to reel under the powerful attacks of a coalition led by Luis Ocaña, particularly on the Col de Porte. Bernard Thévenet won the stage and…Joop Zoetemelk took the yellow jersey, his first in a career that would see him take part in a record 16 Tours de France.

This July 7 would never be forgotten by any of the Tour de France riders, for it was the day that Merckx started to slip. "Nothing will ever be like it was before! Is the Merck era over?", wrote Jacques Goddet. "Merckx couldn't get closer than 80 meters to the leading group. That was where the drama took place. A derisory distance for this king of modern cycling, the greatest champion of all time, who was unable to make up these 80 meters. Reaching the first part of this climbing road, practically touching the wake of those he was chasing, Merckx struggled and struggled, livid. He couldn't take a single inch from their lead. Like a shipwrecked man who starts to lose his head and thrash around crazily, asphyxia started to paralyze him… The gap grew larger. 'The Cannibal' was slowly being devoured."

Up front, the holy alliance of Ocaña, Van Impe, Gösta Petterson, Thévenet, Cyrille Guimard and Zoetemelk forged ahead. At the finish, Zoetemelk took the Tour de France lead by 1 second. Of course, Ocaña was only just behind, waiting for the next day before delivering the death blow. The Dutchman knew it and had no illusions. He just savored his moment.

The previous year, Zoetemelk had suffered on the Cucheron and Porte passes during his first Tour de France. One year later, he took the yellow jersey, after having mastered the very same summits. He was the leader, but for just one day, since on the following stage Ocaña took off for Or-cières-Merlette. But for Zoetemelk, July 7 would remain en-graved forever in his memory even if, later on, he would wear the yellow jersey for 21 days. A jersey that he would take to Paris itself as the victor in 1980.

In 1974, Zoetemelk had reached the height of his powers. But misfortune was awaiting him in the Midi Libre Grand Prix: At Valras-Plage, a badly parked car caused him to crash at full speed. At first it was thought that he had only fractured his petrosal bone, but he was later rushed back to the hospital with a blood clot, and was ill with meningitis for several weeks. It was thought that he would never regain his previous top form, but that underestimated his courage. He again started winning and, in 1976, missed a great opportunity to win the Tour de France. With Eddy Merckx absent from the race and Bernard Thévenet in bad condition, he was the logical favorite, along with Lucien Van Impe. But Zoetemelk was surprised like a beginner by his Belgian rival, who put him 3:18 behind in the general classification, at the end of the great Saint-Lary-Soulan stage in the Pyrenees.

Everything had to be rebuilt from scratch for this ex-speed skater, who was later bothered by a saddle abscess. His tendency was to wait and see what would happen in a race, instead of taking the initiative. Zoetemelk was often re-proached for this attitude, accused—often mistakenly—by his peers of being "wheel-sucker."

He had not worn the yellow jersey since the prologue of the 1973 Tour, when he took it in 1978 in a rather unusual way. At L'Alpe d'Huez, Pollentier was disqualified from the Tour for cheating the anti-doping control and it was Zoetemelk who inherited the golden trophy. But this was Bernard Hinault's first Tour, and the Frenchman snatched the crown from Zoetemelk on the time trial a few days before the finish.

Would his time come around again in 1979? He suc-ceeded in taking the yellow jersey from Hinault on the stage from Amiens to Roubaix, run in part over the cobblestones of the North, after the French star was trapped by various inci-dents. Zoetemelk would lose it in the Alps, at Morzine, once again in the time trial, although he did at least finish second behind Hinault. These two "greats" finished first and second in the final stage on the Champs-Elysées. What a spectacular finale!

Everyone thought that the Dutchman had finally missed his chance of winning the Grande Boucle. By 1980 he was thirty-four: normally the twilight of a cyclist's career.

Joop Zoetemelk fought the best of two generations: After Merckx, he confronted Hinault.

Michael Pollentier has just won the stage from St-Etienne to Alpe-d'Huez, taking the yellow jersey. Alas, he attempted to cheat the medical control and was disqualified from the 1978 Tour.

Podium of the 1987 Tour: Stephen Roche (first), Pedro Delgado (second) and Jean-François Bernard (third).

The Vercors, hotspot of the French Resistance in World War II, also played its part in Tour legend. Roche (right) got away from Bernard, despite the latter's astounding performance, in this 1987 Tour.

Zoetemelk didn't give up though. Still playing a waiting game, he felt strangely serene in the TI-Raleigh team, supported by solid riders who weren't scared of anything. There was an unexpected turn of events. Hinault was suffering from tendonitis and found himself in difficulty several times in the first part of the Tour. It got worse. Zoetemelk won the time trial from Damazan to Laplume, while Hinault could only manage fifth place, 1:39 behind.

Soon the "Badger's" knee gave out on him. The following day, after the stage finish in Pau, he decided to quit, and slipped out of town that night. The way was clear for Zoetemelk, who went on to take the Tour on his tenth attempt.

Two years later, he finished second. When he finally retired at the end of the 1980s, he had one of the best career records in history: world champion, Tour of Spain, 3 time Paris-Nice winner, Tour de Romandie, Blois-Chaville, Tours-Versailles and of course, as we have seen, the Tour de France, in which he took second place 6 times! A very full career, which rewarded an exemplary professional conscience.

Stephen Roche, the brilliant year

Since 1983 he had proven his great professional drive in the Tour de France. He wanted to reach the highest place on the podium by whatever means necessary. The other places didn't interest him. In 1985, he got to third place on the podium. That wasn't good enough for him.

In 1986, the start of his season was wiped out by a crash in the Paris six-day race. The pain of his injured knee caused Roche many weeks of disillusionment. He even considered abandoning his career.

But he returned to his native Ireland, and the suburbs of Dublin. In his heart he heard the warm voices of his friends, of his childhood, voices that had encouraged him when he started out. For their sake, he couldn't suddenly give up. Moreover, his father Laurence begged him to continue, just so that he wouldn't have to return to work at the factory. Stephen remembered the dairy, filling the milk bottles that his father would deliver house-to-house. He slowly got back the use of his gammy knee. It was too late to think about the yellow jersey for 1986. But 1987…

His whole career, or nearly, depended on it.

Six years after his promising professional debut, Roche carried off, as a member of the Carrera team, a triple that before him only Eddy Merckx had managed: Tour of Italy, Tour de France and the world championship. In other words, the pink, the yellow and the rainbow jerseys.

Just to put things in perspective, and before we mention his victorious Tour de France, we should go back to the Tour of Italy, which he managed to win amid great controversy, after a fratricidal battle with his Italian teammate Roberto Visentini. The two men had worn the pink jersey one after the other. Roche then lost it to Visentini on the thirteenth stage, an uphill time trial. Two days later, Roche slipped on a breakaway group so as to, according to him, control the race. But the breakaway continued to gain time, Visentini cracked, and Roche picked up the pink jersey again—which he would keep until the end. The whole of Italy cried scandal, spectaters threw stones at him, and in the Carrera team, Roche was accused of high treason. They turned their backs on him and only the foreigners in his team—the Belgian Eddy Schepers and the French mechanic Patrick Valcke—would still speak to him.

One can well imagine the atmosphere when the team arrived for the Tour de France start in Berlin. This was a very selective Tour without any clear favorites. Roche was one of those tipped to do well, along with the winners of the other big tours: Luis Herrera (Tour of Spain), Andy Hampsten (Tour of Switzerland) and Charly Mottet (Dauphiné Libéré).

The Irishman came to the fore when he won the very long (56.3-mile) time trial from Saumur to Futuroscope. Mottet took the yellow jersey, but the Tour was long and the mountains had yet to come.

In fact, it was another Frenchman, Jean-François Bernard, who was the first to challenge Mottet, on the first Pyrenees stage, accompanied by Dutchman Erik Breukink, and the Colombians Pablo Wilches and Herrera. Roche was lying in third place overall.

The Bernard threat asserted itself on the slopes of Mont Ventoux, in the (22.6-mile) time trial from Carpentras to the summit of the giant mountain. In suffocating heat, Bernard succeeded in taking the yellow jersey by beating runner-up Herrera by 1:30, and taking more than 5 minutes out of Roche.

That left the three stages in the Alps, where the Tour would surely be played out. Everyone expected wide-ranging moves over the hilly roads of the Vercors. A quick glance at the peloton was enough to see that the Colombians were preparing an attack, that Delgado was ready to fire some salvoes, and that the Système U team, with Fignon, was clearly prepared to cross swords with anyone who crossed their path. As for Carrera and Roche, it was essential for them to remain alert if they wanted to grab the biggest slice of the cake.

In 1987, at the La Plagne finish, Roche had gone beyond his limits. This didn't prevent him from reaching the Champs-Elysées with the yellow jersey on his back.

In the 1988 Tour, Pedro Delgado was a big favorite, after his role as Roche's heir apparent in 1987 had given him a formidable desire for vengeance. He prepared for the Grande Boucle like never before.

Delgado's climbing strength quickly put his rivals out of the picture. Apart from the mountains, the Spaniard asserted himself in the time trials and he easily won the 1988 Tour.

The fight for the yellow jersey exploded in this twentieth stage, from Valréas to Villard-de-Lans. At first, it was race leader Bernard who took control, sending off his Toshiba teammates, Dominique Garde, Heinz Imboden and Steve Bauer in the first breakaway group. But at the front of the peloton, Roche was raring to go, always accelerating, particularly on the Col de Tourniol, a climb that was making its first appearance in the Tour de France. It was then that Bernard got a puncture—hardly the best moment—and it was 30 seconds before he was helped out by teammate Jean-Claude Leclercq. For the next 60-odd miles he would always be chasing the leaders—in particular Delgado and Roche—without ever managing to make up any ground. By the finish, he had lost more than 4 minutes, enabling Roche to take the yellow jersey.

But the race was far from over, and the ups-and-downs continued. The next day, Delgado made a long struggle with Herrera on the climb to Alpe-d'Huez. Result: Delgado took nearly 2 minutes out of Roche and snatched the yellow jersey.

The next day, in the Maurienne valley, racing into a violent wind, Roche fought back. Bernard tried to counterattack but soon fell back. Delgado and Breukink, momentarily surprised, caught the Irishman at the summit of the Col de la Madeleine. He would pay dearly for his temerity during the ascent to the finish at La Plagne. Fignon took advantage of the way in which everyone was marking each other to make a bid for the stage. But all eyes were fixed on Delgado and Roche. The latter, tired out by his earlier suicidal breakaway, was 1:30 behind his Spanish rival halfway up La Plagne. Then Delgado, in turn, was in trouble.

At the finish, only 40 seconds separated the Spaniard and the Irishman. Roche fainted as soon as he crossed the line and had to be given an oxygen mask, but by the next day he had recovered.

The suspense continued. Which one, Delgado or Roche, would come out on top? There remained the 23½-mile time trial in Dijon. The Irishman had already proved his strength in this discipline, and he beat Delgado by 61 seconds—Bernard having won the stage—and took the final yellow jersey by 40 seconds.

In this 1987 Tour, Roche had the honor of inaugurating a new yellow jersey. Henceforth, Crédit Lyonnais became the sponsor of the leader's jersey, with its name appearing on the top right-hand side of the shirt, replacing Banania, the previous sponsor.

Pedro Delgado, the tarnished triumph

At the start of the 1988 Tour, Pedro Delgado benefited from favorable predictions for two main reasons. First of all, his role as Stephen Roche's heir apparent in 1987 gave him legitimate hopes of victory. Losing a Tour de France by 40 miserable seconds creates a formidable desire for vengeance, particularly since he was far from being outclassed by the Irishman in that 1987 Tour. Second, Delgado had prepared for the '98 Tour as never before. He knew the extraordinary fascination that the Tour had for the Spanish, so much so, that the members of parliament even suspended a session, in 1987, to watch his triumph on the slopes of Alpe-d'Huez!

In Spain, everyone had eyes for him alone, since his national rivals were not up to par: Alvaro Piño seemed too inconsistent, Pello Ruiz-Cabestany appeared too limited in the mountains, Julian Gorospe didn't meet the hopes that had been placed in him and Marino Lejaretta was at the end of his career.

Delgado was ready, well prepared by the Tour de Romandie and the Tour of Italy. In this Tour, which he would win, he started to turn heads in the first mountain stage from Besançon to Morzine which passed by Lake Geneva. Jean-François Bernard blew up on the first big climb, while the other favorites moved to the front: Delgado, Mottet, Herrera, Hampsten, Breukink, Urs Zimmermann, Steven Rooks, Gert-Jan Theunisse and the Colombian Fabio Parra—who then launched a savage attack, forcing Derlgado to throw himself into a headlong chase.

The most appreciated quality of the Spaniard was his watchful eye. Like some feudal lord, he let whom he wished break away or, if he considered them to be too much of a threat he quickly reeled them in. This was the first great demonstration of Delgado's capacities, which had passed unnoticed by most observers, but which revealed his qualities nonetheless.

On the second day in the Alps, he again rose above his direct opponents, placing himself right behind the unstoppable Dutchmen Rooks and Theunisse at L'Alpe d'Huez. That was when he took the yellow jersey, to never let it go. The following day, in the uphill time trial from Grenoble to Villard-de-Lans—thirteenth stage—over a course that favored the all-arounders rather than the pure climbers, he beat the best time, set by Bernard, by 44 seconds. A wonderful victory, which no doubt heralded another. Happy with himself, the racer from Segovia calmly headed for the anti-doping control. From then on, a whole other story started to unfold.

After the Alps came the Pyrenees. At Guzet-Neige,

The yellow jersey dwarfed by the grandeur of the Tour.

Delgado won the 1988 Tour. Suspected of using a steroid-masking drug, he kept a disarming silence on the matter. No matter, he became the third Spaniard to win the Tour.

The blond and smiling supremacy of the Dane
Bjarne Riis (Hautacam, 1996).

Delgado allowed himself the luxury—behind the early break-aways—of another blisteringly fast final mile. He left everyone in the last 200 meters and strengthened his grip on the yellow jersey. A derisory gain in time, for sure, but what a psychological blow!

Struck by his ease, authority and determination, his potential rivals again gave in to him on the main Pyrenees stage over the Tourmalet, before the finish in Luz-Ardiden. Never in difficulty, Delgado handled events perfectly, facing competitors who were already beaten. Thousands of Spaniards crossed the border to acclaim Don Pedro, without knowing that in just a few hours time the storm-clouds would be rumbling.

It all started on the evening of the stage finish at Bordeaux, while the crowds slowly left the course after a relatively unimportant stage. The television channel Antenne 2 let slip the rumor that Delgado had tested positive at an anti-doping check. The news, made official the following day at 12 p.m., concerned the urine sample he had given after the Villard-de-Lans time trial. A second analysis was requested and, that very evening, the yellow jersey was cleared. There had been a trace of a suspicious substance in the analysis: probenecid. This was a diuretic that could mask the presence of anabolic steroids. It was not a doping product, that was certain, but the International Olympic Committee had put it on its list of prohibited substances precisely because the presence of probenecid in a sample implied the absorption of doping products. Probenecid was not yet on the list of banned products of the International Cycling Union, however.

Delgado saved his yellow jersey and became the third Spaniard in history to win the Tour de France.

Bjarne Riis, as Indurain starts to fade

It was 1996: for the first time in history, a Dane would find victory in the Tour de France. His name? Bjarne Riis, virtually unknown in the sporting world. Third at the 1995 Tour and fifth in 1993, he had toiled in the shadows for a long time in support of team leaders. It must be said that his self-sacrifice, his discretion and his long silences, all of them supreme qualities of a born lieutenant, were much appreciated.

Riis finally decided to play his own cards at the 1996 edition. First, though, he had to evaluate the form of the solid favorite, five-time winner Miguel Indurain.…

But things had already clicked into place for the Dane, allowing him to better evaluate both men and events. It came during the Tour the previous year, in Belgium, on the demanding time trial course between Huy and Seraing.

In the searing heat, the astounding Riis was leading the yellow jersey at all the intermediate time checks, and he was still ahead, as they drew closer to the finish. Indurain, informed of the danger, had to pull out all the stops in order to win the stage by a handful of seconds.

Riis thought that a great lesson could be learned from this close call. The moment of reckoning would come later though, since this 1995 Tour once again saw an Indurain victory.

Riis must have been thinking about it on July 6, 1996, which took him and his companions from Chambéry to Les Arcs, with the finish at an altitude of 5577 feet. But those thoughts came only at the last moment, because when the 10-mile climb toward the finish began, Indurain was still at the front with him, along with Tony Rominger, Richard Virenque, Abraham Olano, Alex Zülle and Luc Leblanc. About 3½ miles from the finish, Leblanc broke away. Of little threat to the general classification, they let him escape. Behind him, the pace wasn't slackening either. Suddenly there was a unique sight…. Indurain dropped back to the rear of the little group.

At 2½ miles from the summit came the kill. Indurain lost contact and would finish in a total daze. At the finish, Indurain was 4:19 behind. He had already lost the Tour, even if he still forced himself to believe in his ability.

Riis finished seventh at Les Arcs, and moved up to fourth place in the general classification, just 8 seconds behind the new leader, the Russian Eugeni Berzin. Riis now awaited his moment, backed by his magnificently well-structured German team, Telekom, which he had joined at the beginning of the year, after several seasons spent with Fignon at Système U and Berzin at Gewiss.

Slowly but surely, the Dane wove his web. After Les Arcs, he finished second behind Berzin in the Val-d'Isère time trial, and moved up to second place on general classification.

Riis knew the Russian's inconsistency, and believed that he could take him whenever he chose. In any case, the stage from Val-d'Isère to Sestriere by way of the Iseran, Galibier, Montgenèvre and Sestriere climbs seemed to suit the Telekom rider better.

Nobody yet knew that the course would change. Due to bad weather conditions over the Alps, the race organizers decided to eliminate the first part of the stage for safety reasons. The giant Iseran and Galibier passes were no longer included in the course and the stage distance was reduced to just 28½ miles: up to Montgenèvre doom a short descent, before a climb to the finish in Sestriere, at an altitude of 6676 feet.

The public's loyalty to the Tour, year after year, is unfailing.

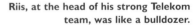

Riis, at the head of his strong Telekom team, was like a bulldozer.

A wonderful all-round cyclist, Riis was an expert at damage-control in time trials. In the 1996 Tour, the Viking added panache to his great achievements, winning two stages in the mountains. This had not been done since Laurent Fignon in 1989.

A straightforward and model team rider before he stole the limelight, and winner in 1996, Riis brought a certain romanticism to the glory of the Tour.

From the foot of the Montgenèvre, that is to say shortly after Briançon, the Dane attacked. His lead was never more than 50 seconds, but what mastery! Harmonious and nicely balanced in his movements, he drove his powerful muscles right up to the Piazza Agnelli in Sestriere, despite a lightning counterattack by Leblanc and Virenque, who took second and third place. Berzin lost contact with the chase group less than 2½ miles from the summit, and the yellow jersey slipped from his shoulders to Riis's, never to leave them.

The Dane was ready to respond to any attack, but none came, neither in the Vercors nor in the crossing of the Massif Central. There remained only the Pyrenees starting with the climb to Hautacam, at the end of the sixteenth stage.

The Dane's rivals very quickly showed themselves. At 4½ miles from the finish, while the little group of favorites climbed with successive accelerations, Riis had the audacity and presumption, to let himself slip back to the rear in order to judge the state of fatigue of his rivals, an astounding and surreal sight that had never been seen before. He thus realized that Berzin had already reached his limit, that Indurain was about to let go, that Rominger was out of it, and that Virenque was not the rival that he had been led to believe. Strengthened by this information, as if a computer was telling him how to proceed, Riis accelerated while his rivals all blew. Now he was on his own, definitively on his own.

The yellow jersey added panache to the exploit, having now won two mountaintop stage finishes, something that had not happened since Laurent Fignon in 1989.

The seventeenth stage from Argelès to Pamplona, as beautiful as it was, only served to confirm the strength of the man in yellow. His rivals were now only racing for second place. Mass had been said and, in Pamplona, they could only salute, in his hometown, a Miguel Indurain who was admitting defeat. All in all, a transfer of power.

Jan Ullrich, a fiery temperament

The young German Jan Ullrich, a former world champion, finished in second place at the 1996 Tour de France, behind his teammate Bjarne Riis. Ullrich actually defeated Riis to win the fiercely contested twentieth stage, a time trial, from Bordeaux to Saint-Emilion.

In 1997, Ullrich was ranked as a favorite, but was hardly convincing that season, having stayed away from the major events. The previous year, he had declared: "From now on, the Tour is the sole objective of my career." As for Riis, apart from winning the Amstel Gold Race, where he proved to be supremely powerful, he had avoided difficult tasks. Ullrich didn't lose time in asserting himself in the '97 Tour. He finished second in the Rouen prologue, 2 seconds behind Englishman Chris Boardman. That didn't say everything, but it was enough to reveal the intentions of the young German, who had one major asset: his punch in the time trials.

It was on the stage from Luchon to Andorra-Arcalis that Ullrich finally let rip. At the start of the stage, Riis was still number one on the Telekom team, but the 1996 Tour winner was no match for Ullrich on the tough Arcalis climb. Their directeur sportif Walter Godefroot, was still backing both horses, but he was now leaning toward the young German and instructed him to attack.

Ullrich needed no persuading on that climb to the finish. He accelerated, gripping the bottom of the handlebars. The style of this kid from the old East Germany remained fluid in spite of the effort. The commentators, always easily excited, immediately thought they saw a new Koblet or Merckx in this young German. His face bore no sign of pain. In a single 6-mile climb, he had annexed the Tour de France.

Marco Pantani and Virenque were expected to shine on a stage like this, but they were laid low by a young rider who was, more than ever, the specialist of the solo effort. Everyone else was KO'd: Francesco Casagrande, Laurent Brochard, Laurent Dufaux, José Maria Jimenez, Fernando Escartin and even his teammate Riis. A star was born. The yellow jersey had fallen to a supreme talent. Some riders were not far from repeating the words of Géminiani, in 1951, on the day that Koblet exploded on the stage from Brive to Agen: "If he continues like that, then we can all go home, we won't win anything else."

At this point, the day before the Alpe-d'Huez stage, the toughest climber, Marco Pantani, was 9:11 behind the yellow jersey. But wasn't Richard Virenque a threat, at 5:42 behind? "He's already too far back…", shouted the German rider to Godefroot, very sure of himself. He was so sure that he eased off a little and let Pantani break away to the Alpe-d'Huez summit. But the Italian took only 47 seconds off him.

What could be done to beat Ullrich? Virenque was not yet finished. He received a telephone call in his room after the stage, which assured him that Ullrich had fallen victim to food poisoning and so wouldn't be up to scratch the following day on the stage from Bourg-d'Oisans to Courchevel, via the Glandon, Madeleine and Courchevel passes.

At the Festina team's dinner table that evening, the

The moment when the 1997 Tour could have changed course. Jan Ullrich found himself isolated by an attack from Virenque and his men. In the Maurienne valley, he had confidently waited for his teammate Riis, who helped the German close the gap (Bourg-d'Oisans to Courchevel).

On the 1997 Tour's Colmar-Montbelliard stage, Ullrich found his supporters in a sea of German flags. For the cyclist from the old East Germany, the coronation was not far off.

**Ullrich, uncontested
winner of the 1997 Tour.
He was the first German
to win the greatest race
in the world.**

**Ullrich has caught Virenque and the two of them started
their ascent toward Courchevel. Virenque confirmed his
climbing skills and Ullrich his all-round ability.**

riders, having been told this news, decided to attack on the first pass.

The spectacle was well worth watching. As soon as they began climbing the Col du Glandon, Virenque and his teammates were on the move and the fight was in full swing. Gian-Luca Bortolami, Neil Stephens, Christian Moreau, Didier Rous, Pascal Hervé and Brochard led a peloton that soon fell apart. At the Glandon summit, the count was easily made. Twenty-odd men scrambled over it together, with Ullrich the only one remaining from his team.

The leaders then descended to the Maurienne valley. Downhills were the yellow jersey's Achilles heel. Ullrich had trouble finding the right lines in the turns. At only twenty-three years old, he still had things to learn. On the contrary, when confronted with pure climbers, he knew how to pace himself, so as not to run on empty—proof of a wonderful lucidity.

But downhills were not one of Ullrich's strengths. He nearly overshot a bend on the Glandon descent while following in the wake of the Festina men. The German understood that in this little game, and with a whole team against him, he risked making a fatal mistake. Intelligently, he decided to wait for his teammates Riis and Bölts to catch up. Virenque and his team thus took a 1:35 lead, not really that big, considering Ullrich's 6 minute lead over Virenque in the general classification.

But it was only after a long chase with Riis over the Madeleire that the yellow jersey caught Virenque, shortly before Moutiers. There remained the climb up to Courchevel. Both men finished together, with Virenque taking the stage in the sprint.

It was fortunate that the Tour was nearly over for Ullrich, since he was highly stressed and under constant pressure, as was proved in the stage through the Vosges mountains. On the ascent of the Hundsrück pass he conceded a minute, but Virenque's Festina team did not receive a single offer of collaboration and a majestic Ullrich made a strong comeback. The Tour was now definitively his.

Pantani finally at the summit

At the end of the 1997 Tour, a long reign was predicted for Ullrich. However, underlined Jacques Augendre in the *Livre officiel du Tour de France,* "the Tour is not for rent and one cannot reserve the yellow jersey like one might book a holiday villa. Jan Ullrich is perhaps a meteorite like Hugo Koblet, with great fluidity and a 'silent' pedal stroke."

That was certainly something one had to be careful of, for the following winter the young German, his success having gone to his head, neglected his preparation and found himself worryingly overweight at the start of the 1998 season. In the very first races he discovered how futile his efforts were. The peloton either broke away without him or else left him at the side of the road in the middle of a race. Distressing, to say the least. Ullrich continued—as did his directeur sportif—to affirm that he would be ready for the Tour de France. The doubts set in, though.

Everyone awaited the prologue of the Tour with impatience, held that year in Dublin, in an atmosphere poisoned by the doping scandal surrounding the Festina team.

Boardman won the prologue—a foregone conclusion—in front of Olano, while Laurent Jalabert, Bobby Julich, Moreau and Ullrich shared third place, 5 seconds behind the winner.

So Ullrich had made a strong showing and prepared his assault on the yellow jersey. The winner of the 1997 Tour and his teammates had already focussed their attention on the seventh stage, a time trial from Meyrignac-l'Eglise to Corrèze (36 miles). The predictions proved accurate and Ullrich, in the lead at all checkpoints, won it, with the American Tyler Hamilton 1:10 behind, Julich 1:18 behind and Jalabert 1:24 back… The Tour, which had only just got going, already seemed destined for Ullrich—especially when the Festina team, with Zülle, Dufaux and Virenque, was thrown out of the race.

It was rumored that Ullrich was now left without a single rival up to his measure. But how could one affirm this so early on? The Tour was only at the end of its seventh stage. This was something that the main contender and the whole of his team were well aware of, and that was why the yellow jersey let a six-man breakaway shoot off toward Montauban the following day, an exploit that achieved its goal, with the yellow jersey going to the young Frenchman, Laurent Desbiens.

The race now headed into the Pyrenees, at last giving an opening for the climbers—especially Marco Pantani, who had won the Tour of Italy the previous month. The first of the Pyrenees stages ended at Luchon.

Everything became clear on the day's last major challenge, the Col de Peyresourde. At the beginning of the pass, with the Italian Rodolfo Massi alone up front, Ullrich lit the tinderbox, with a strong attack. Olano and Jalabert dropped back, but Pantani quickly counterattacked, to finish second behind Massi and snatch 23 seconds from Ullrich—who had won back his yellow jersey.

1998 Tour. Pantani follows Ullrich, on the Madeleine attempting to prove that the mountain was above all his domain.

Pantani, followed by Bobby Julich the revelation of the 1998 Tour. With the Italian's victory, the hour of the pure climbers was back.

Against all the odds, the 1998
Tour de France crowned
a true climber: Marco Pantani.

In this tormented Tour, in spite of the doping
problems, Pantani had now found his way.

The boisterous Pantani now found himself on his terrain of predilection, with the finish of the tenth stage situated on the plateau de Beille, at a height of 5731 feet. Ullrich prepared himself for a difficult day, since he knew that Pantani was targeting that ten-mile climb for another attack.

An accurate prediction. At exactly 7½ miles from the finish, the Italian climber shot off like a meteorite, overtook all the riders who had broken clear on an earlier climb, and won the stage.

Curiously, in the last few hundred meters, the yellow jersey lost contact with Julich, Michael Boogerd and Christophe Rinero who were accompanying him up till then. Perhaps Ullrich was paying for the effort of too rapid a return after a puncture at the foot of the final climb? Ullrich had clearly panicked.

At any rate, even though the German hung on to the yellow jersey, in 24 hours Pantani had taken 2:03 off him and climbed back to 3:01 from him in the general classification.

There remained the Alps, which Ullrich dreamed of during the transition stages. But doubts had set in. He started to worry, even if he didn't show it. Partly because of the rebellious climate that had settled on the Tour after some new doping scandals.

The great day arrived on July 27, and great and grandiose it certainly was. The weather certainly set the scene: persistent rain, cold and fog. This time, Pantani didn't want to wait for the mountaintop finish of this fifteenth stage from Grenoble to Les-Deux-Alpes. With just a 5½-mile final climb it appeared to be a risky undertaking. But the earlier climbs over the Croix-de-Fer, Télégraphe and Galibier passes helped to sort things out. About 3½ miles from the summit of the Galibier, and 30 miles from the finish, Pantani made two probes before launching a strong breakaway. Ullrich crumbled immediately. From then on, in the icy rain and thick fog, one could distinguish two kinds of trains: an express train shooting toward the finish and a puffing locomotive which strove and hooted to reach the top of the mountain. Pantani was now set to win the Tour de France. Winner in Les-Deux-Alpes, and the new yellow jersey, he finished the stage 8:57 ahead of Ullrich.

"Elefantino"—as he was nicknamed—was now bursting with exhilaration. Ullrich could do nothing about him, even though he regained 2:35 in the time trial between Montceau-les-Mines and Le Creusot. The Italian won the Tour with a 3:21 lead over the previous year's winner, thus completing the Tour of Italy-Tour de France double in the same year, the seventh man ever to carry off such an exploit.

Armstrong or the lesson of life

With Pantani and Ullrich absent, a new reign began in 1999, that of the American Lance Armstrong. The Texan, who had escaped from the clutches of a rampant cancer, returned to competition in 1998 with a morale of steel. After several encouraging performances, his entourage persuaded him that he could win nothing less than the Tour de France. So with the cold determination that characterized him, the American prepared his challenge with training camps in the mountains, to reconnoiter all the passes; one already felt that he was on target.

Armstrong won the Puy-de-Fou prologue and took the yellow jersey, in true American style, on the Fourth of July! The strongest rider in the field, he won the Metz time trial a few days later and then won the first major mountain stage, in Sestriere, under an overcast sky, before going on to control the running of things in the 3 other major mountain stages. Final victory was his. The 1999 Tour had only two yellow jerseys: JaanKirsipuu on the flat, and then Armstrong, a situation not seen since 1977. What a demonstration of his determination.

Throughout this Tour, Armstrong gave a great lesson in life as well as a great lesson of sport.

But this wasn't enough for him. He wanted to prove that this first Tour victory was neither a fluke nor dishonestly won. The 2000 race would serve as the confirmation of his success and total resurrection. As if there was any doubt!

Everything rolled sweetly in the prologue with the Texan finishing only two seconds behind the Scotsman David Millar. He had lost nothing of his redoubtable time-trialing qualities. More proof of this came in the 43½-mile team time-trial between Nantes and Saint-Nazaire. Herculean Armstrong was too strong for his teammates and broke the cohesion of the U.S. Postal team, a dangerous thing, for Lance would need all his men…

As soon as the mountains appeared, Armstrong ripped through the Tour like a tornado. At the Hautacam summit, Ullrich and Zülle, his major rivals, were more than three minutes behind.

Mont Ventoux was certainly less favorable to him and he slipped back toward Pantani and let the Italian win the stage, but the Alps didn't cause any great upset to the general classification, and the time trial between Freburg-im-Brisgau and Mulhouse allowed the yellow jersey to set a new record for a time trial longer than 30 miles, by averaging 33.471 mph. No further comment is necessary…

Cancer survivor Lance Armstrong
took ownership of the Tour
in 1999 and 2000.

Kings for a Day

Kings for a day, a lifetime's dream

Jules Buysse preceded his brother in the conquest of the yellow jersey, winning the first stage of the 1926 Tour. His brother Lucien would go on to win that Tour.

Maurice Archambaud built a large part of his career on track records (including hour record in 1936). An excellent road-racer, he won 10 stages of the Tour de France and wore the yellow jersey for 13 days.

Previous: Nicolas Barone, the ephemeral yellow jersey. A wonderful story was unfolding for him, as the yellow jersey allowed him to win the battle of his love (1957 Tour).

During the 1920 Tour, Félix Gœthals had the privilege of sharing the yellow jersey with his compatriots Thys, Nottiat, Rossius and Masson for two stages.

T he dream of every Tour de France cyclist is to wear the yellow jersey for at least a day. Even if the reign is ephemeral, to lead the Tour de France for a few hours in a golden garment brings you everyone's notice. When the peloton passes, the yellow jersey is pointed out to children as an example of deserved success.

Here are a few of these "ephemera", who inscribed their names in the annals of the Tour de France.

The true peak of Romain Bellenger's career started with the return of cycling after the 1914-18 war. A sturdy fellow at 5 feeet 11 inches, he was a worthy rival, in build and ardor, for the Pélissiers, Alavoine and Christophe.

Having only recently joined the professional ranks in 1921, Bellenger soon became the best French rider at the Tour, but he drank some icy spring water and, suffering from diarrhea, was forced to withdraw on the Portet-d'Aspet Climb.

In spite of the yellow jersey, which he took in 1923 at Sables-d'Olonne, his reign was short lived. He hung on to his trophy for two days, until the foot of the Pyrenees, but the competition was too much for the man whom Henri Desgrange nicknamed "the Wader-bird."

This was also the period of a good-looking chap, unpolished but generous, named Ferdinand Le Drogo who wouldn't hear of sacrificing life's pleasures for cycling asceticism. He was strongest in the discipline that called for the fewest tactical subtleties, the time trial.

A companion of Francis Pélissier in the 1927 Tour de France, whose first few stages were run as team time trials, he made it a point of honor to conquer and then defend the yellow jersey while crossing his native Brittany, creating indescribable enthusiasm in Dinan (fifth stage) and Vannes (seventh stage); but he didn't defend it any farther, having considered he'd fulfilled his duty.

A little later, Léon Le Calvez was another friend and protégé of Francis Pélissier. Also from Brittany, he always

showed his authority in a race, and was particularly clear-headed. He took the yellow jersey in 1931 at the end of the stage from Dinan to Brest, and so he too crossed Brittany as leader of the Tour.

Maurice Archambaud was another Frenchman to make an impact. Even though it was his world hour record that made his name, he was also an authentic Tour rider. In his first participation, in 1933, he won the first stage, took the leader's jersey and kept it until the end of the ninth stage. He finally lost it when he blew up on the Col de Vars, and the Belgian Lemaire took over the lead.

Of strong character, though not very communicative, Archambaud returned to the Tour in 1936 to again wear the yellow jersey after a brilliant start. He wore it all the way to Grenoble but, as before, he hit a bad patch in the Alps.

In 1939, the race had five leaders, of which the first yellow jersey went to Amédée Fournier, a rapid sprinter. Coached and trained by Francis Pélissier, Fournier came from the track school of cycling. Belgium's Romain Maës replaced him briefly as leader, but on the half-stage from Vire to Rennes, the Breton Jean Fontenay, son of a hard-working family of farmers and fishermen from Saint-Servan, demonstrated an extraordinary brilliance. With his teammate Eloi Tassin, he attacked from the start, sowing panic in the peloton. Tassin won the stage and Fontenay took the yellow jersey, to cross Brittany as a conquering hero, before ceding his trophy to René Vietto. That was the start of another story.

The startling début of Vietto in the 1934 Tour de France soon earned him the title of "King René." This popularity was immortalized when he gave his wheel to Antonin Magne, his team leader, whose wheel had been wrecked in a crash.

Vietto took the yellow jersey for the first time in 1939, at the finish of the stage from Brest to Lorient. The duel which he fought with the Belgian Sylvère Maës then filled the crowds with excitement. After having dominated in the Pyrenees, Vietto reached the Alps with a lead of less than 2 minutes over the Belgian. Isolated, the man from Cannes foundered on the Izoard, opening up the way to Maës.

Then came the war.

The dream of Jacques Marinelli took shape at the start of the 1949 Tour. Selected for the second time in his career, he wore the jersey of the Ile-de-France team. He showed his mettle in the second stage, finishing second in Brussels behind the Belgian Roger Lambrecht. Attacking constantly, he had no fear of banking. In the fourth stage from Boulogne

VIETTO'S BROKEN DREAM

In 1947, René Vietto took the race lead in Brussels after a lone breakaway that he started 50 miles from the finish. Was his long attack enough to win the Tour? "We hoped so," wrote Jacques Goddet, "against the convential wisdom of the Tour de France." Vietto lost his lead to the Italian Ronconi for two days in the Alps, but took it back in Digne. Behind him, Robic started to gnaw away at his lead. Three days from the end of the Tour, at the start of the interminable time-trial stage from Vannes to Saint-Brieuc, Vietto still wore the yellow jersey, but, drained by constantly defending his narrow lead, he crumbled. His dream had come to an end.

Fiorenzo Magni wore the yellow jersey in 3 Tours de France. In 1950, the sudden withdrawal of Bartali would force him to leave the Tour while still leading the race.

At the start of the 1949 Tour, Jacques Marinelli (third from the right) never imagined that he would become the great revelation of this Tour.

The attacking qualities of Bernard Gauthier were rewarded in the 1950 Tour de France by a yellow jersey that he would keep for 7 stages.

to Rouen, Marinelli slipped into a group of sixteen riders which would eventually unravel.

In Rouen, he finished alongside the sturdy Lucien Teisseire who won the stage. But Marinelli took the supreme honor. "Our parakeet has become a canary," wrote the Tour director. The nickname stuck, as did the yellow jersey, for many stages, since he rode prudently, profiting from the intense rivalry of the two Italian super stars Fausto Coppi and Gino Bartali. Another Italian, Fiorenzo Magni, would snatch the lead in the first Pyrenees stage. Marinelli had a wonderful adventure and fought on, finishing third in the final classification, having succeeded in latching on behind the two *campionissimi* and winning the hearts of the crowds.

He popped up again in a beautiful breakaway at the start of the 1950 Tour, but suffered from boils and had to quit on the seventh stage. That same day, the yellow jersey was taken by Bernard Gauthier, a courageous fighter of incomparable generosity, who defended it valiantly until Pau with his teammates of the Sud-Est team. Nicknamed "Lion Heart", Gauthier also became known as "Monsieur Bordeaux-Paris," following his four victories in that wonderful endurance race.

The 1951 Tour had seven leaders. Apart from those whom we have mentioned in the course of this book, we couldn't leave out Roger Lévêque who deposed the Italian Serafino Biagioni at the Rennes finish and held the lead for six stages. This ex-deportee had certainly earned this recompense after having won the fourth stage, from Le Tréport to Paris, on his own.

Gilbert Bauvin also briefly took the yellow jersey in this Tour, succeeding the Dutchman Wim Van Est—who abandoned after falling into a 200-foot ravine in the Pyrenees. Little Bauvin, dogged and brave, developed a taste for the golden emblem, succeeding another Dutchman, Wont Wagtmans as leader of the 1954 Tour, in Luchon. It was again a brief reign, as he lost the lead when taken by surprise on the stage on the rolling roads of Causses. The cyclist from Lunéville again won the leadership in 1958. A member of the French team, he fought from the start and got his reward, but for one day only, in Caen.

Nello Laurédi was Bauvin's contemporary and without doubt one of the most talented riders of his era. He became a naturalized Frenchman in 1948 and had just settled in Provence. Did he have the means to win the Tour de France? He found it hard to complete twenty-two stages without weakening, but he excelled in the week-long Dauphiné

Libéré, which he won three times. Lauredi wore the Tour yellow jersey just once, in 1952, at the finish of the stage from Le Mans to Rouen, after a wonderful breakaway in the company of his teammate and friend, Gauthier.

This was the time of the development of national and regional teams, which projected such personalities as Roger Hassenforder, who became Tour leader in Caen in 1953, his first participation. Quite a character, both on and off a bike, Hassenforder, yellow jersey for five stages, was pure class personified. He would win eight stages in six Tours, but would never find the yellow jersey again.

In that same Tour de France of 1953, the longest reign was that of Jean Malléjac. A slender cyclist, boosted by a solo victory in the fifth stage from Dieppe to Caen, this Breton felt an ambition growing in him that irritated his team leader Jean Robic. Robic took the yellow jersey in Luchon, after a long solo break, passed it to Francis Mahé the following day in Albi, after having trapped the French team. The next day, on the Albi-Béziers stage, the national team launched a commando operation to annihilate these "incorrigible Bretons." Unfortunately for the French team, Mallejac had slipped into the breakaway and took the yellow jersey, which he would keep until the Gap-Briançon stage, starting point for Louison Bobet's Tour de France victory.

In 1959, one of the team riders on the Centre-Midi team, Henry Anglade, had a great opportunity to win the Tour. He finished second overall to Frederico Bahamontes, who was well protected by the French team that united to prevent a regional rider winning.

Anglade obtained a certain legitimacy when finally selected for the French team in the 1960 Tour. He took the yellow jersey in Caen, but had to hand it over to the Belgian Jean Adriaensens, after Anglade's own teammate, Roger Rivière, initiated a four-man break on the road to Lorient; with Gastone Nencini, Adriaensens, Hans Junkermann and Roger Rivière carving out a quarter of an hour lead for themselves over the peloton.

The public always loved the story of a "nobody" taking the yellow jersey. That was the case of the Parisian Michel Vermeulin in 1959. He was blessed with a state of grace from the very start of the Tour, participating in numerous breakaways, notably on the stage to Roubaix, where a 10-man group took 11 minutes off the stars. In the Pyrenees, Vermeulin found the highest reward of his professional career, when he donned the most beautiful of jerseys. He was one of the first to reach the summit of the Col du Tourmalet, and set

Hassenforder launched into the 1953 Tour at vertiginous speed, taking the yellow jersey in the fifth stage. On the ninth day of the race, worn out, he missed a vital break and lost his lead.

Jean Malléjac. In the 1953 Tour de France, he kept the yellow jersey for 5 stages, until Louison Bobet took the mantle from him in Briançon.

THE CLASS OF ANTONIN ROLLAND

During the "Louison years," a particular niche was held by Antonin Rolland. Nicknamed "Tonin the Taciturn," he had an exemplary career. A high-class cyclist, with an excellent spirit of self-sacrifice, he was one of Lousion Bobet's adjutants in the Tour. He had great success in 1955. Taking the yellow jersey in Metz, after having won the selective

stage from Dieppe to Roubaix, he wore the emblem for 12 stages. Discreet to the point of self-effacement, he was never to acquired the confidence that could have enabled him to become one of the greatest French champions.

"Thank you Father, God will reward you." (Henry Anglade, Tour de France 1959).

The finish in Bagnères-de-Bigorre was, for the novice Michel Vermeulin (right), the greatest day of his life. André Darrigade (left) had to content himself with the green jersey (1959 Tour).

The unknown Italian, Tomasso de Pra, has just dispossessed his teammate Rudi Altig of the yellow jersey (1966). The German doesn't seem to hold it against him.

about defending the yellow jersey with unexpected vigor, keeping it through the following stage, in Saint-Gaudens, and the day after that, where he led a successful breakaway with the Swiss Rolf Graf, to Albi.

His reign came to an end though, on the treacherous stage from Albi to Aurillac through the Cévennes.

In 1966, the Tour experienced some unexpected developments, due to the Anquetil-Poulidor rivalry. In the Pyrenees, a young Italian by the name of Tomasso de Pra, teammate of Rudi Altig with Molteni, won the stage from Bayonne to Pau and took the yellow jersey. He was dispossessed the following day, in the major stage from Pau to Luchon, by Jean-Claude Lebaube from Rouen, with victory being fought out between him and the German Karl-Heinz Kunde. Lebaube brought much satisfaction to Louis Caput, directeur sportif of the humble Kamome-Dilecta team.

The Belgians Willy Van Neste and Jos Spruyt both discovered the honor of the yellow jersey in 1967, as did the Frenchman Raymond Riotte who became leader for a day in Strasbourg, after having slipped into a profitable breakaway. It was not far from there that Charly Grosskost from Alsace, the French pursuit champion, took the first yellow jersey of the 1968 Tour, winning the prologue—just as he had done at Paris-Nice and the Tour of Italy that same year. He won again the following day in Esch-sur-Alzette; but on day three could not prevent Belgium's Herman Van Springel from snatching his trophy, at the end of a half-stage team time trial, where the Belgian team asserted its collective force.

Next in line that year was Raymond Poulidor's faithful retainer, Jean-Pierre Genet. What could be more touching than seeing this Breton, seemingly hewn from Armorican granite, adorn himself for just one day with the prize that was forever forbidden to his master. Genet gave way in Bagnols de l'Orne to Georges Vandenberghe. This ex-assistant-butcher from Bruges, "obliging both by nature and by profession," in the words of Pierre Chany, was selected for the Tour in order to prepare Walter Godefroot's field sprints, which he did with zeal. Vandenberghe would make the most of the peloton's apathy and kept his jersey until the sixteenth stage.

The following year—1969—saw the coming of Eddy Merckx. He very quickly allowed his teammate Julien Stevens to make his acquaintance with the yellow jersey, while, even quicker—for a single day—the Breton Désiré Letort put his nose in front. A most controversial chap this Breton from Plancoët, Letort was disqualified from the French Road Championship in 1967, after a positive drugs test.

The three day was reign of José Catieau from Picardy, who then passed the yellow jersey to his leader Luis Ocaña—whom he helped, as best he could, to win the 1973 Tour.

The courageous José attacked on the opening road stage from Rotterdam to Saint-Nicolas, won the stage and took the yellow jersey two days later on the road from Roubaix to Reims, while he accompanied Ocaña over the cobblestones of the North in a nine-man breakaway. Catieau kept the jersey until the seventh stage, when his captain Luis took command of the Alps.

A long-time protagonist at the Tour was Raymond Delisle, who took part 12 times. He had always played the role of a mover and shaker, once attracting the wrath of Roger Pingeon, who accused him of riding too often just for himself. On a certain 14th of July, 1969, with the French champion's jersey on his shoulders, Delisle went off to chase a symbolic victory in Luchon. As for the yellow jersey, he would wear it only at the end of his career, in 1976. The action took place in the Pyrenees, which would play the pivotal role in this Tour. The first mountain stage took the riders from Port-Barcarès to Pyrenees 2000. Delisle, knowing these parts well, made an attack on the Col de Jau, but his initiative left the peloton rather indifferent. Van Impe held back, respecting the instructions of his directeur sportif, while the Gan-Mercier team had a mission to protect Poulidor. Delisle thus profited from this situation and won the stage, and took the yellow jersey he so richly deserved. The favorites had lost nearly 7 minutes. Delisle held onto his trophy the following day, during a transition stage which arrived at Saint-Gaudens, but lost it to Van Impe the next day in the famous Pla-d'Adet stage, over the Menté, Portillon and Peyresourde passes.

1978 announced the arrival of Bernard Hinault. In his first Tour, his teammate Jacques Bossis would realize his dream of taking the yellow jersey. He managed it at the end of the longest stage of the Tour, from Saint-Amand-les-Eaux to Saint-Germain-en-Laye (151 miles), which he finished in second place behind the German Klaus-Peter Thaler. But an intermediate sprint during this stage had earned him a 20-second bonus. That was enough to make Bossis race leader.

The following year, another of Hinault's teammates, Jean-René Bernaudeau, found fame in the first stage from Fleurance to Luchon. Hostilities opened in the rain between the Menté and Portillon passes, with René Bittinger and Bernaudeau leaving a breakaway group to finish together. Bernaudeau took the yellow jersey by 4 seconds. The follow-

First yellow jersey of the 1968 Tour, Charly Grosskost from Alsace won the prologue, as he had already done in Paris-Nice and the Tour of Italy (left, future Tour director Jean-Marie Leblanc; right, Michel Grain).

Georges Vandenberghe took the yellow jersey in the fifth stage of the 1968 Tour. His reign was limited, although he did make it as far as Albi, end of the sixteenth stage.

In the 1968 Tour, Herman Van Springel grabbed the yellow jersey in the third stage. But his final ambitions seemed more serious. He lost it, took it back and only lost it definitively on the last day.

In the 1976 tour, a close struggle opposed Raymond Delisle (yellow jersey for 2 days) and Raymond Poulidor for third place. Poulidor's experience eventually won the day.

In 1984, Vincent Barteau had a long reign in
the yellow jersey. Before ceding the mantle
to his teammate Laurent Fignon, he had to face
the harassment of Hinault (left).

A prologue specialist, the Norman Thierry Marie conquered
the yellow jersey in 3 of them (1986, 1990 and 1991).

ing day, his team leader won the stage and the jersey, but what a heady souvenir for Bernaudeau!

Vincent Barteau, on the other hand, had time to get used to his glory. It all started on July 3, 1984, during the fifth stage from Béthune to Cergy-Pontoise.

The Portuguese Paulo Ferreira had launched the offensive, almost as soon as the flag went down. Maurice Le Guilloux responded and caught up with him. As for Barteau, he found himself in fifth position in the peloton. He also attacked, not realizing what he was letting himself in for, and caught the two breakaways. The three men soon carved out a lead over the rather apathetic peloton. At mile 55—the stage consisted of 128½—the trio had a 20-minute lead. The gap reached 24:46 at its maximum at mile 71. By the finish, it was down a little to 17:41, with the sprint going to Ferreira, and the yellow jersey to Barteau.

From then on, a dream week opened up for Barteau. He realized very quickly that he could take this yellow jersey far, very far, and started to get attached to it. He admitted: "It'll be tough when I have to give it up." In the Pyrenees, he finished among the first twenty at the Guzet-Neige summit and astounded everyone by latching onto team leader Fignon's breakaway from the leading group at only 1½ miles from the line, a completely unexpected performance.

Barteau finally had to let go of the jersey on the high mountain stage between Grenoble and Alpe-d'Huez, finishing nearly twelve minutes behind the winner Herrera, while Fignon took the lead, never to let it go.

One could draw a similarity between Barteau and another Norman, Thierry Marie, the first yellow jersey of the 1986 Tour, who rode with the aid of then new technology: an aerodynamic, low-profile frame with integral handlebars. He didn't cause a surprise in winning the Boulogne-Billancourt prologue, as he had won the prologues of the Tour of Spain and the Tour de l'Aude the same year.

Marie's team, Système U, controlled everything in the early stages, including the team time trial from Meudon to Saint-Quentin-en-Yvelines. Marie picked up the yellow jersey again—after having lost it in the morning stage to the Canadian Alex Stieda—and before ceding it the next day to his teammate, Dominique Gaigne. Gaigne kept the jersey for only one day, whereas Marie had not yet finished with it. He would have to wait for 1990, however, before making a real comeback. "Monsieur Prologue," as the Italians called Marie, brilliantly asserted himself again at the prologue in Futuroscope, leaving Greg Le Mond 4 seconds behind. He kept it for only one day, but came back the following year to win another prologue in Lyon. Nobody was surprised. His director Cyrille Guimard might well have shouted out to him, during the race, that "it'll be a close thing," but the Norman benefited from the last few hundred meters to change from a 54 x 13 to a 54 x 12 gear, sensing that it would be a close finish. But he was further ahead than he thought and beat Erik Breukink by 2 seconds.

Marie had another surprise up his sleeve that year: a long solo breakaway—138½ miles—between Arras and Le Havre. He won the stage and took back the yellow jersey, and crossed his native Normandy as Tour leader. Marie then lost the lead to LeMond in the time trial between Argentan and Alençon. His yellow reign was definitively over. It's interesting to note that, in his last victory, Marie's bike—fitted with state-of-the-art aero' bars—handlebars that cost 600,000 francs, the same as his annual salary.

His teammate Charly Mottet also took the yellow jersey, in 1987, in the 54-mile time trial between Saumur and Futuroscope, which was won by Stephen Roche. That year, the team director's tactic was to accompany the attacks. Mottet's teammate Martial Gayant followed this instruction to the letter, slipped into a long attack led by Kim Andersen, and snatched his comrade's yellow jersey.

The Pyrenees arrived and the commitment was as strong as ever. As the top climbers battled it out, Mottet got back on track and took the leader's position again. He dug deep into his reserves and, the next day, at the finish on the Luz-Ardiden summit, he still kept the jersey. But Mottet's resources were starting to wear thin. He had kept the lead for five days, until the arrival of Jean-François Bernard, who had made good progress through the Pyrenees. They now reached Mont Ventoux, which was climbed as an individual time trial. Bernard threw himself into it, without thinking about the next day. In the first part, before the ascent of the mountain itself, he was already credited with the best time. It seemed as if he had set off too quickly, but he continued to close the gap between himself and Herrera, Delgado and Roche, whom he slowly caught, Roche having set off three minutes before him. Bernard failed to catch him by just 41 seconds. It was a wonderful exploit. "Bernard, Hinault style" headlined *l'Equipe* eight columns wide. But the next day Roche and Delgado surprised him after a puncture.

Three years later, in 1990, Ronan Pensec from Finistère came strong in the Alps, taking the yellow jersey at the end of the tenth stage from Genève to Saint-Gervais Le Bettex.

The yellow reign of Charly Mottet lasted for 6 days (Tour de France 1987). His great talent deserved more.

Martial Gayant, winner in 1987 of the eleventh stage from Poitiers to Chaumeil...and the yellow jersey.

Ronan Pensec, hero of the first stage of the 1990 Tour, raced after the yellow jersey for much of the race. As soon as the road started to climb, in Saint-Gervais, he grabbed it for 2 days.

In spite of his victories in the world championships and the French championship, Luc Leblanc would wear the yellow jersey for only 1 day, in Jaca, during the 1991 Tour.

The Breton had led the very first breakaway of the Tour and really took the limelight once they reached the mountains. Heroic on the Alpe-d'Huez climb, the time trial between Fontaine and Villard-de-Lans proved fatal to him, however, and he ceded the yellow jersey to one of his breakaway companions from the first stage, the Italian Claudio Chiappucci.

For Luc Leblanc, the "Yellow" hour struck only once, in 1991. Leader of the Castorama team, this native of Limousin demonstrated stamina that one didn't expect from him. In the Pyrenees stage from Pau to Jaca, he took the yellow jersey, but a breakaway by Chiappucci and Miguel Indurain the next day condemned him to finishing the stage on his own, more than 10 minutes behind the two escapees. Leblanc confirmed his progress in this Tour by finishing fifth overall, the second Frenchman in the final classification. Richard Virenque also experienced just one day of yellow jersey delirium, in Pau, after the only Pyrenees stage of the 1992 Tour, between San-Sebastian and Pau.

The ensuing reign of Pascal Lino in the yellow jersey would last much longer. A native of Morbihan with a flowing style from the track riding school, he infiltrated a long breakaway between Pau and Bordeaux and found himself in first place overall, with a little less than 2 minutes over his RMO teammate, Virenque, and 6 minutes over the third place man, Indurain himself! Considering that Virenque had been wearing the yellow jersey at the Pau start, Lino hadn't exactly helped the progression of the breakaway.

From then on, Lino demonstrated a superb level of performance, his situation making him the objective ally of Indurain. He kept his beautiful jersey for 10 days running, even allowing himself the luxury of attacking on the slopes of the Col de l'Iseran in the thirteenth stage, at the end of which, in Sestriere, he gave up his trophy to Indurain.

In 1992, the Swiss Alex Zülle seemed destined for a prestigious career, when he became leader of the Tour for the first time in his life, at the end of the first stage in San-Sebastian. But his reign didn't last, ending the next day in the Pyrenees. Much was expected of Zülle, but he would only take the leader position again in 1996, in the 's-Hertogenbosch prologue, in the Netherlands. It was as if he was once more proclaiming his ambitions, but again he lost the jersey very quickly and dropped out of the limelight following a fall in the Alps during the seventh stage.

In the meantime, in 1995, Jacky Durand from Mayenne got a taste of the highest honor in the storm-affected Saint-Brieuc prologue. The prologue favorite Chris

Boardman, who had started at the end of the day, threw caution to the winds and slammed into the crash barriers after skidding through a particularly difficult bend. Durand was the unexpected winner and took the yellow jersey. Luckily for him, his start early in the day meant that he had raced on a dry circuit. He crossed the Côtes-d'Armor between Dinan and Lannion as leader, before ceding to Laurent Jalabert who started his reign in Vitré, but for only 2 days. It was his best Tour ever.

The leaders' waltz continued in 1995 with Ivan Gotti, the winner of the Tour of Italy, leading in Le Havre and Dunkirk, Riis in Charleroi and Johan Bruyneel in Liège.

The hemorrhage of the yellow jersey came to an end with the Seraing time trial in Belgium, where Indurain brought the mayhem to a close.

The Northerners certainly seemed to have the wind in their sails. In 1998, Laurent Desbiens took the yellow jersey on the ninth day of the race, after the stage from Brive to Montauban. Riding in a breakaway group with Durand and five others, Desbiens's teammate, the powerful Philippe Gaumont contributed to the success of the breakaway and the Northerner's yellow jersey, a jersey that he kept until the foot of the Pyrenees. The reign of the climbers was commencing, and the glory of the yellow jersey continued.

Laurent Jalabert. Although only moderately successful in the Tour, he remains one of the few competitors to have worn the three jerseys of the three great Tours (France, Italy and Spain).

Richard Virenque, lifetime subscriber to the polka-dot jersey of the King of the Mountains, took the yellow jersey for just one day, in Pau, in 1992.

THE PANACHE OF CÉDRIC VASSEUR

In 1997, the Northerner Cédric Vasseur became a legend on the stage from Chantonnay to La Châtre, between the deep Vendée, and the Vallée Noire evoked by George Sand.
He took a long solo breakaway of 91 miles to a victorious conclusion. The yellow jersey was waiting for him at the end of the road. His maximum lead, 62 miles from the finish, was 17:45. 20 years beforem in Felsberg, his father had also won a stage on his own. In 1997, Vasseur would defend his mantle 5 days. Nearly at breaking point in the Andorra-

Arcalis ascent, at the end of the tenth stage, with his yellow jersey hanging only by a thread, Vasseur gallantly launched a final attack, 8 miles from the finish. It was a great show of his offensive spirit and his obstinacy, but he lost the yellow jersey at the finish.

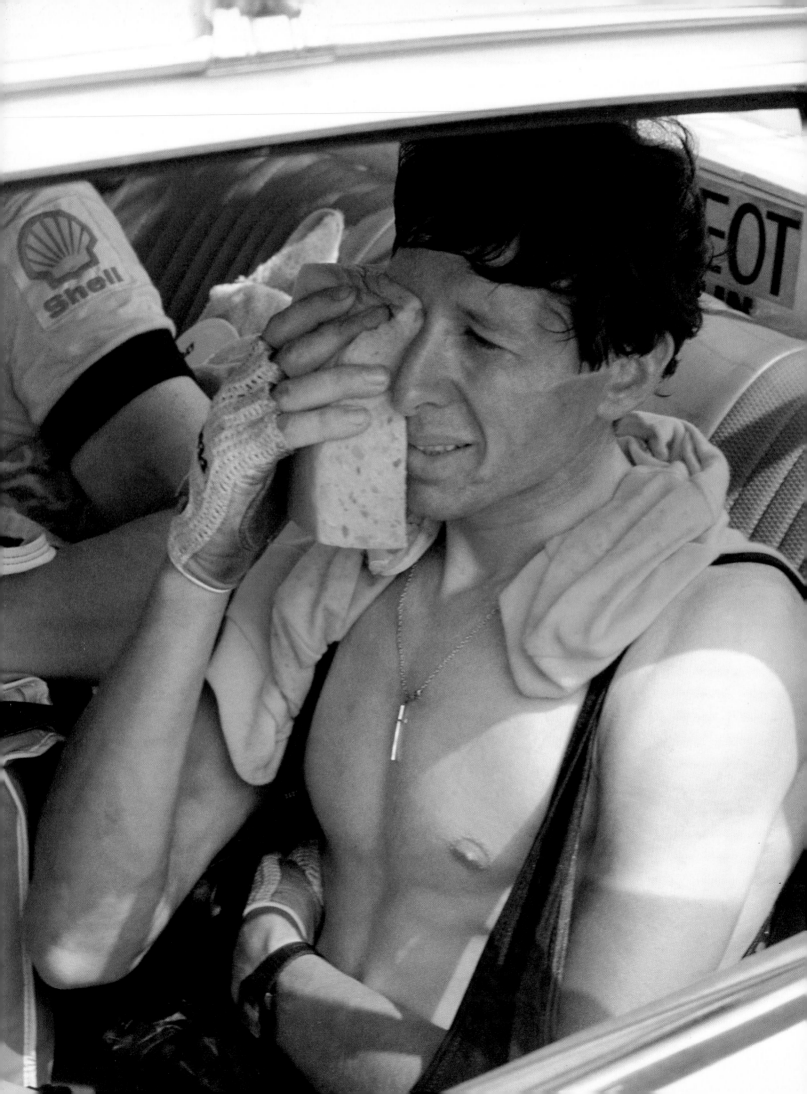

Ups and Downs

The dark side
of the golden mantle

Jean Alavoine on the Col de Peyresourde,
at the 1922 Tour.

Previous page: Pascal Simon, beaten by pain,
has just taken off his yellow jersey, crying over
a Tour de France victory that once seemed
inevitable (1983 Tour).

Robert Jacquinot, twice winner of the first stage of the Tour
(1922 and 1923) and…twice leader.

At the start of the 1920s, Robert Jacquinot and Jean Alavoine were considered potential winners of the Tour de France. Alas, they came up against men of character like Henri Pélissier and Ottavio Bottechia, but the French public still held them in high esteem.

Both men wore the yellow jersey in 1922, while Jacquinot agaiin started well the following year. He broke away in the Côte de Fécamp and became the first yellow jersey, but lost it on the second stage.

Alavoine, too, repeated a feat he performed in 1922: winning both the mountain stages in the Pyrenees. On 1923's first major climb, the Aubisque, Bottechia showed his class by reaching the summit first, in front of Alavoine. Jacquinot fought back hard behind these two leaders, with Pélissier hot on his heels. And Jacquinot passed Bottechia a mile from the summit of the Tourmalet, but suddenly weakened. But that was only the start of the day's drama, which was played out on the Peyresourde.

His eyes rolled upward, Jacquinot pedaled onward, still leading the race, but he wasn't able to swallow any food. At the end of his tether, he collapsed on the side of the narrow dirt road, and stretched out in the ditch. When he recovered his senses sufficiently, he got up, pushed his bicycle in front of him and climbed up the last slopes on foot.

That was when Alavoine caught up with him and called out to him: "So, Robert, something wrong? You struggling?" Jacquinot, haggard, looked at his comrade and, still with enough strength to take his cap off, he murmured: "Good day, Johnny boy, it's worth [a try]…"

A few minutes later, reinvigorated by the bracing mountain air, Jacquinot regained his strength on the descent, but Alavoine was long gone, and won the stage a quarter-hour in front of runner-up Jacquinot. It was not the same in the Alps though, where Pélissier took over, while Alavoine crashed heavily and couldn't take the start in Briançon. His hour had passed, as it had for Jacquinot. Pélissier and Bottechia had now taken center stage.

Fiorenzo Magni tormented

In 1950, Fiorenzo Magni's performance was near faultless, and it was only due to outside circumstances that he lost the yellow jersey. Already, the previous year, he had taken the lead on the first mountain stage, from Saint-Sébastien to Pau. He kept it for the whole crossing of the Pyrenees and would only lose it in the Alps, in Briançon, to his compatriot Gino Bartali.

In the 1950 Tour de France, riding for the Italian national team, Magni took the yellow jersey again, at the end of the stage from Pau to Saint-Gaudens, a stage which was won by his team leader, the steadfast Bartali.

Those are the facts, but at this point in the tale, we should recount the true goings-on of this sunny day in the Pyrenees.

Jean Robic attacked near Eaux-Bonnes, to tackle the Aubisque. At the summit, Bartali was a minute behind the quartet that was chasing Robic, who shot off far ahead. Bartali then made up the time on the Tourmalet, and caught Louisoon Bobet and the others.

Then came the Col d'Aspin, which held some grave consequences for the Tour. At the summit there was a crash, and Bartali declared that he had been punched by some fanatics. Bobet was an important witness to this: "A swerve, due to the presence of a press motorcycle, caused us to collide. Bartali was on the ground as well as me. I don't deny it," continued Bobet, "that the Italians had been insulted during the ascent of the Aspin. With all the passion of which they are capable, the spectators' faces were a little threatening, because of their anger when the Italians came by. Still, I think I can state that, during the few seconds that it took to free us from our bikes, Bartali was not struck. And I think that I would be correct in saying that what he took for hostile gestures, even believing them to be blows, were above all, as often happens, attempts to be the first to help him back onto his bike."

At the finish in Saint-Gaudens, Bartali outsprinted a small peloton to take the stage victory, while Magni took the yellow jersey. The Italians won across the board, but a few hours later, there was general astonishment: The Italians announced that they were quitting the Tour!

Race directors Jacques Goddet and Félix Lévitan rushed to the Hôtel de France, in Loures-Barousse, where the Italians were staying. Goddet started off timidly: "I assure

Bartali, king of the Pyrenees, won the stage from Pau to Saint-Gaudens. His compatriot Magni finished with him and took the yellow jersey. That evening, the Italians quit the race (1950 Tour).

Bartali quits the Tour with all his teammates, including Magni, the yellow jersey. The Tuscan, who declared having been struck by some firebrands on the Col d'Aspin, remained inflexible: "I withdraw!" he said. Magni never got to actually wear his leader's jersey, it went straight into his suitcase (1950 Tour).

The yellow jersey in the ravine. The Dutchman Wim Van Est fell more than 100 feet while descending the Col d'Aubisque. He had a miraculous escape. They knotted tires together and pulled him out. He got away with a few broken ribs.

At the start of the stage from Dax to Tarbes in the 1951 Tour, Van Est (left) received encouragement from the Swiss Hugo Koblet.

you, Gino, that in spite of what I admit are unfavorable appearances, the French public does not agree with these hooligans who dishonored themselves this afternoon. Last year, we didn't lump together the few agitators in Aosta with the whole of the Italian nation."

Bartali put down his cigarette and sighed: "I don't want to risk my life because of some madman, even if he is the only one of his kind."

As for Magni, the yellow jersey, he reasoned that it was in his interest to follow suit. "I'm with Gino," Magni said simply, as he folded his yellow jersey and put it in his suitcase.

A yellow jersey in the ravine

The following year, 1951, the Pyrenees were the scene of another drama. The man involved was Wim Van Est, a sturdy Dutch road racer from North Brabant. A squat man, solidly built, and a strong rider, this smiling character had made his first appearance in cycling at age twenty-four. Two years later, he found himself at the start of the Tour de France.

Van Est took his place on the Dutch national team. He showed strong form, slipped into breakaways and displayed a promising ability. On the twelfth stage, the day after Koblet's famous attack on the stage from Brive to Agen, the Dutchman infiltrated a strong, attacking group of 10 men, and won the stage. He also took the yellow jersey.

The following day, the Tour tackled the Pyrenees. Van Est had never seen them, let alone climb them. He didn't even know how to climb a mountain pass let alone descend one. He was certainly not the only one, but he was the leader of the Tour de France after all. The ascent went quite well, but on the twisting downhill he was taking bad lines through the turns. Soon he didn't seem to know where he was or whom he was chasing. Near the Balcon du Soulor, with the steep precipice to the left, another false maneuver threw him into the ravine. The yellow jersey came to rest more than 100 feet down. The Belgian racer Roger Decock witnessed the scene, losing himself in confused explanations to his directeur sportif, Sylvère Maës, who didn't understand a thing he said. Then Dutch rider Gerrit Peeters arrived and realized the severity of the situation. His teammate Wim had fallen into a chasm 150 feet deep. Those following, petrified, didn't dare look over the edge of the precipice. And yet, he had to be rescued. They then thought up a clever solution: they tied together a chain of tires and pulled him out. They had a fortunate surprise: his injuries were only slight. Taken to the hospital in Tarbes with some broken ribs, he stayed there only briefly. His hour of glory had come.

The affair was splashed across the newspaper. A particularly ingenious Dutch copywriter came up with a slogan that was all the rage in the Netherlands: "I fell 200 feet, my heart stopped beating, but my Pontiac still ran."

Pascal Simon, struck down in the heart of it

Thirty-two years after Wim Van Est, another yellow jersey found himself thrown to the ground: Pascal Simon, who deserved to win the Tour that year, he was so dominating.

On July 19, 1982, on the heights of Orcières-Merlette, where he had just edged out Pierre-Henry Menthéour for stage victory, Pascal Simon, winner of the Tour de l'Avenir the previous year, had let slip that in 1983 he would tackle the Tour with serious ambition. He already wanted a leader's place on the Peugeot team.

And the '93 Tour started out for him well: second in the team time trial, he got across the cobblestones of the North remarkably well. And so he was in sixth position in the general classification when he tackled the Pyrenees.

On the stage from Pau to Luchon, after the Aubisque and Tourmalet passes had set the race in motion, Simon left the peloton on the first bends of the Col d'Aspin. He overhauled several groups and launched himself into the conquest of the yellow jersey. By the summit of the Col de Peyresourde, he was in third place on the road, with a 3-minute lead over favorites Jean-René Bernaudeau and Laurent Fignon.

At the finish in Luchon he became leader of the Tour.

"One can't promise anything," he said, "but today I took a major step toward final victory."

Alas, the following day, on the stage from Luchon to Fleurance, Simon was victim of a crash near the town of Lannemezan. It seems that it was caused by his teammate Bernard Bourreau, who fell just in front of him. At the finish, Bourreau claimed: "It was Jonathan Boyer who elbowed me, and caused me to crash." As for Simon, he didn't accuse anyone. When the X-rays showed a hairline fracture in the left shoulder blade, he commented soberly: "I am prepared to suffer." He didn't know how right he was. For 5 stages, he impressed the public and all the race followers with his courage. Every morning, his soigneur wrapped the yellow jersey's back with bandages from neck to waist, then the Peugeot leader put on his golden tunic with extreme precaution. "So a yellow jersey can actually feel pain?" asked Henri Haget

Tour de France 1983: the stage from La Tour-du-Pin to Alpe-d'Huez. Pascal Simon, injured, stops. Yellow jersey for a week, he pedaled with a fractured shoulder blade after a crash.

ROLF SÖRENSEN, PLEASURE AND PAIN

In 1991, at the start of the team time trial in Lyon, the big favorites were the Spanish ONCE team and the Dutch PDM squad. Nobody bet a dime on the Ariostea team and hardly anyone else on Castorama. Still, the Italians of Ariostea, thanks to some formidable riders and doubtless also to the startling way that team director Giancarlo Ferretti led his men, put on a real show. Later on, the Castorama boys gave the illusion, through some good time splits, of doing even better. But the enormous work of Fignon was not enough to beat Ariostea. So Ariostea's Danish star, Rolf Sörensen, took a yellow jersey that seemed promised to Greg LeMond or Erik Breukink. The Dane personified the modern champion par excellence, through the aggression and class that he demonstrated when it came to the crunch. Sörensen's father was his son's strongest supporter, interrupting his vacation to travel to Lyon, where, in the afternoon, he saw his son take the first yellow jersey of his career: *den gule troj*, as it's called in Danish. Sörensen defended his jersey with ardor over the next few days, hoping to keep it until the individual time trial stage, on the ninth day. But after an unfortunate crash 2½ miles from the finish of the sixth stage in Valenciennes, he was diagnosed with

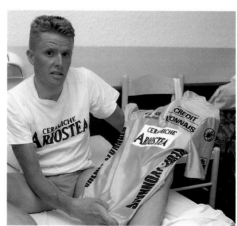

a fractured collarbone. Sörensen insisted on finishing the stage, but couldn't start the following day.

Stéphane Heulot added the Tour yellow jersey to his French champion's jersey in 1996. A wonderful season for the man from Rennes.

The yellow jersey is sometimes cursed: Heulot was obliged to withdraw from the '96 Tour in the Alps, suffering from tendonitis.

in *Vélo* magazine, also mentioning another piece of gallantry: the feed zones, where his teammate Frédéric Brun assisted him. When Simon was thirsty, Brun helped him drink.

On Monday July 18, at 1 p.m., at the top of the Little Côte de la Chapelle-Blanche, Simon finally gave up, yet no mass would be said in memory of the defunct yellow jersey. Neither wreaths nor flowers. Everything happened with the utmost discretion and with Dr. Porte of the race organization as sole funeral director. Simon reached Alpe-d'Huez by ambulance, without either sirens or flashing lights. He had given his all and could no longer pull on the handlebars.

Heulot, the honor and hardship of French cycling

The year is 1996. Everything started with the French road championship. Stéphane Heulot took the tricolor jersey and from then on tried to honor his title in every competition. And why not in the Tour de France, too? He had already learned a great deal from Miguel Indurain, when riding for the Banesto team. In 1996 he belonged to the Gan team and awaited his moment. On the fourth stage, between Soissons and the Lac de Madine, in Lorraine, he slipped into a breakaway shortly after Fère-en-Terdenois. 25 miles had been covered, with exactly 120 left.

Five men were in the break: Heulot, of course, but also Wilfried Nelissen, Rolf Jaermann, Mariano Piccoli and the young Cyril Saugrain from the humble Aubervilliers 93-Peugeot team.

Over roads through the famous vineyards of Champagne, scene of so many wartime battles, the 5 breakaways achieved a maximum lead of 17:40, at about 60 miles from the finish. This first, wonderful breakaway of the 1996 Tour seemed to promise great things.

After 144 miles of racing, the 5 contested the final sprint on the banks of the tranquil Madine lake, with their lead over the peloton now out to 4:33. The young man from the Paris suburbs, Saugrain, proved to be faster than Nelissen, but Heulot had taken the yellow jersey.

His jersey was well-soaked the next day on the stage from the Lac de Madine to Besançon, which linked Lorraine to Franche-Comté. But the atrocious weather forced many a rider to withdraw and Heulot was suffering from tendonitis. How would he get through the mountains?

The seventh stage, from Chambéry to Les Arcs—the first major alpine stage—took the race over Madeleine and Cormet-de-Roseland passes before the ascent to Les Arcs. A crazy stage was in the making. The weather didn't improve either, raining incessantly, and in the space of this wet afternoon, events unfolded with an relentless rigor.

On the Col de la Madeleine, Laurent Jalabert unexpectedly blew up, and Heulot began to flag a little. The riders had hardly covered 43 miles, with he toughest 80 left to go.

Small groups formed after the descent on the valley road toward Albertville. The upcoming Cormet-de-Roseland peaked at an elevation of 6456 feet. Heulot called Dr. Porte, the race doctor. His knee was stopping him from pedaling. Near the top of the pass, the wearer of the yellow jersey pulled to the side of the mountain road. He set foot on the ground and couldn't continue. His directeur sportif Roger Legeay rushed up to him, but the man from Rennes was crying for not being able to defend his lead in the mountains.

Chris Boardman, the double curse

It was always at the brightest point that Chris Boardman saw his dream crumble. In the 1998 prologue through the streets of Dublin, he didn't disappoint his fans, covering the 3½ miles at an average speed of 33.653 mph; and, with three victories in the prologue (1994, 1997 and 1998), he holds the three best prologue times in the history of the Tour de France.

In 1995, he could also have won the prologue in Saint-Brieuc. Brittany was flooded by storms, but the Englishman shot out of the starting gate like a rocket, swept through two or three bends at breaking point—a true acrobat—and went full tilt into the next, longer curve. Moving too fast on the wet, downhill turn, his rear wheel skidded out and Boardman veered into the metal barrier on the right. Roger Legeay's car, which was following, just missed him. Result: multiple fractures to the ankle, injuries to the forearm and multiple contusions.

His Tour was already over before it had even begun.

Chris Boardman in full flight.

THE ACROBAT'S FALL

In 1998, Chris Boardman won the prologue and took the yellow jersey. At the end of the first stage, he profited from the battle of the sprinters, to hang onto his yellow jersey. The following day, from Enniscorthy to Cork, another acrobatic battle was expected at the finish. Alas, in the 93rd mile of this 127-mile stage, just before the peloton prepared to dispute a bonus sprint, Boardman touched the wheel of Frédéric Moncassin, causing him to crash violently. With injuries to the face and elbow, and a crack in the left radius, Boardman was taken by ambulance to the Cork hospital. Some saw the terrible hand of fate, since he quit the Tour on July 13, anniversary of the death of Tom Simpson. He was also the thirteenth wearer of the yellow jersey in history to be forced to quit.

Boardman took his first yellow jersey in 1994. He would wear it twice more.

Tightrope Walkers

Treading the high wire

Rafaele Di Paco

Rik Van Steenbergen, a legend of both road and track cycling, took the yellow jersey in the 1952 Tour. But the Belgian's ambition's lay elsewhere. Pity...

Previous page: The typical sprinter of the new generation, the Tuscan Mario Cipollini, yellow jersey, locks horns with the German Erik Zabel, green jersey in the points classification and just as swift as the Italian.

André Darrigade, the sprinter par excellence, won 22 stages of the Tour de France, using his remarkable burst of speed, seen here flying clear of Ferdi Kübler (right) and Stan Ockers (Bordeaux, 1954 Tour).

Road-sprinters are the aristocracy of cycling, always attracting the admiration of the general public. These men, who race with power and virtuosity, do not, in general, find ultimate victory in the Tour de France. But in the early stages, a victorious sprint may well be rewarded with the yellow jersey.

Between the wars, two men fought a merciless sprint battle with each other, the Italian Rafaele Di Paco and the Frenchman Charles Pélissier.

A true king of stage victories in the Tour of Italy (15) and the Tour de France (11), the Tuscan's preeminence never failed in his sixteen-year career. His most impressive exploit came during his first Tour de France, in 1931, when he wore the yellow jersey for 4 days, from Vannes to Bayonne.

He shared the leader's jersey with Charles Pélissier, his direct rival, in Sables-d'Olonne, before the latter snatched it from him on the stage from Pau to Luchon. Heir to the famous Pélissier name, Charles was the younger brother of Henri and Francis, and led a true revolution in cyclists' posture. He would never show himself in public unless his appearance was perfect. Much of his popularity was due to this attitude.

He took the yellow jersey for the first time, in 1927, by winning the first stage.

The Belgian Rik Van Steenbergen also won a first Tour stage and the yellow jersey in 1952, on the stage from Brest to Rennes. Having broken away with his compatriot Maurice Blomme and the Frenchman Pierre Pardoën, he beat them in the sprint. The Belgian kept the jersey the following day, then discreetly disappeared a few stages further on. He made his name in the one-day classics and remains a cycling legend, on both the road and track.

From time to time, Van Steenbergen rubbed up against Miguel Poblet, one of Spain's greatest champions, but, like the Belgian, he wore the yellow jersey in just one Tour, in 1955. This followed his winning the opening stage

André Darrigade, during the first stage of the 1956 Tour, has just taken the yellow jersey. Even within the French team, he still had to fight hard to prove that he was a worthy leader.

from Le Havre to Dieppe, at the head of a 10-man break. He was thus the first Spaniard to wear the yellow jersey.

The Swiss Fritz Schaër attempted to beat him a few times, but without success. A contemporary of Kübler and Koblet, Schaër was considered the third man of Swiss cycling in its golden age. Not only was he the first ever winner of the Tour de France points classification (green jersey) in 1953, but he also occupied the race leader position that same year, from the first to the fifth stage, winning the first 2 stages.

André Darrigade was one of the most remarkable French road-racers. During his career this man from deep in the Landes region preferred the all-or-nothing of crazy "nose into the wind" rides. He had the generosity and taste for panache of a true leader. His famous turn of speed didn't hurt the feelings of the men working hard in a breakaway, since he put so much heart into it himself.

An indispensable member of the French team in the 1950s and '60s, he won 22 Tour stages, taking his first yellow jersey in 1956, at the end of the first stage from Reims to Liège. He won the opening stage 4 times in a row, from 1956 to 1959, and thus the first yellow jersey. All in all, he wore it for 19 days.

Darrigade's Béarnais neighbor, Robert Cazala, rode with him on the French team in 1959 at the height of its internal Anquetil-Rivière rivalry. Cazala, without really wanting to, benefited from the quarrel. Putting to good use a wonderful breakaway on the cobblestones of the North he won the third stage from Namur to Roubaix, and took the yellow jersey, which he showed that very evening, with great respect, to his roommate Louison Bobet. Cazala defended the lead for five stages, finally losing it on home territory, in Bayonne, to the sturdy Belgian Eddy Pauwels.

Another Frenchman with a fine burst of speed was the Breton Joseph Groussard, who amassed a copious pile of loot, including the 1962 Milan-San Remo. He also won the yellow jersey in 1960, in Dieppe, despite losing the stage to the Italian Nino Defilippis.

His brother Georges Groussard had his own glory days in 1964, when he wore the yellow jersey for 9 stages before ceding it to Jacques Anquetil. "What are you planning on doing with all this money," the journalists asked little Georges. "Aren't you worried about it going to your head?" He usually answered: "To my head, no! Quite simply, I'm scared of not sleeping as well, for money keeps you awake and that makes you grumpy."

While the Belgian Rik Van Looy was a fine example

Third stage, from Namur to Metz, of the 1959 Tour. Although Bernard Gauthier leads Fernand Picot and the breakaway group here, Roberr Cazala, in fourth place, is already preparing the victory that will earn him the yellow jersey.

1962 Tour. The German Rudi Altig (left) and Darrigade passed the yellow jersey back and forth to each other at the beginning of the race.

Rik Van Looy was only an ephemeral leader of the Tour de France. In 1963, he won the Parc de Princes stage, beating his compatriots Bevoni Beheyt and Robert Lelangue.

A TOUCH OF LUCK

Cyrille Guimard got his chance in 1972, when he wore the yellow jersey for 8 stages. His fabulous turn of speed helped him to win four stages, including 2 in front of Eddy Merckx. Knee problems obliged Guimard to withdraw from the race.

of power and fighting spirit, this "King of the Classics" wore the yellow jersey only once in 7 Tours. He won 379 victories in 17 years of professional cycling and is the only cyclist to have known success in every major race in the international calendar.

The year of his yellow jersey—1962—was also the year of his crash into a motorcycle on the eleventh stage, from Bayonne to Pau, which handicapped him for the rest of his career. In Bordeaux, two days before the crash, he had the pleasure of seeing his number one teammate, Willy Schroeders, also take the yellow jersey for a few days.

Another of Van Looy's teammates, blessed with a lovely burst of speed, Ward Sels, took the yellow jersey by winning the first stage of the 1964 Tour.

Two years before, Germany's Rudi Altig did the same thing, winning the opening stage in Spa, and taking the yellow jersey for the first time in his first Tour de France. Twice in 3 days he relegated the élite of the road-sprinters, the second win giving him back the yellow jersey that Darrigade, had taken from him in Herentals.

Altig would also have the honor of taking the yellow jersey at home, at Freiburg-im-Brisgau, during the 1964 Tour. In 1966, he kept it for nine days, after winning the first stage. He remains one of the people to have won the leader jersey in the 3 grand tours.

Altig's compatriot Rolf Wolfshohl didn't have this chance. He was Tour leader for a single day in 1968, before being deposed by the Spaniard Gregorio San Miguel.

Patrick Sercu, a friend of Eddy Merckx, won 7 stages in two Tours. In 1974, he wore the yellow jersey at home in Belgium, at Harelbeke, and won the Tour points classification that year.

Like Sercu, Italy's Francesco Moser made his name in the classics and on the track. But he never played a major role in the Tour. He took the first yellow jersey of the 1975 Tour by winning the prologue, but was dispossessed of it by Merckx on the sixth day of the race, in the time trial at Merlin-Plage.

At this time, Freddy Maertens became the number one sprinter. In 1976 he won the prologue, like Moser had done the year before, keeping the yellow jersey until the mountains, at Alpe-d'Huez. Maertens was above all an aficionado of the green jersey.

After the Belgian, the German Didi Thurau came to light in 1977. At twenty-three years old, this cyclist with the physique of a top model, won the prologue, shone in the

Freddy Maertens, yellow jersey after winning the prologue of the 1976 Tour, took 3 stage wins in mass sprints to keep the leader position for 10 days.

Pyrenees, then held the lead for 2 weeks, taking the yellow jersey back home to Germany. Alas, he very soon became a six-day cyclist, preferring cash to glory on the road.

In 1978, Dutchman Jan Raas won the yellow jersey in the prologue, before outsprinting Maertens and Jacques Esclassan the next day for another stage win, and another maillot jaune. His powerful Raleigh team, managed by Peter Post, won the team time trial from Evreux to Caen and retrieved the yellow jersey, which had been stolen the day before, in Saint-Germain-en-Laye, by Hinault's teammate, Jacques Bossis. This time it was the German Klaus-Peter Thaler who inherited it, before passing it on to another teammate Gerrie Knetemann—who would also win the prologue in Fleurance the following year.

Among the best sprinters of the 1980s, the Belgian Eric Vanderaerden held a choice place. Yet he took the yellow jersey only twice. In 1983, first of all, he won the prologue in Fontenay-sous-Bois. Yellow jersey the first day, he kept the trophy the next day before ceding it to the excellent fighter, Jean-Louis Gauthier. In 1985, he lost the Plumelec prologue to Hinault, but took the yellow jersey from him the following day, at the end of the first stage, from Vannes to Lanester, which was won by Rudy Matthijs. Vanderaerden crossed Brittany in yellow, before losing his leader position in Normandy. He was an excellent one-day classic rider.

His compatriot Wilfried Nelissen asserted himself in the 1993 Tour, in Vannes, winning both the stage and the yellow jersey. That year, the Italian Mario Cipollini succeeded him on the fifth day of the race, not after a spectacular sprint, but, paradoxically, following a team time trial from Dinard to Avranches. The Tuscan's team—GB-MG—won the stage and Cipollini himself kept the famous knitwear until the seventh stage.

After the reign of Cipollini, that of Belgium's Johan Museeuw began in the seventh stage, but the following day's time trial at the Lac de Madine saw him lose it to Indurain.

Museeuw returned in 1994, for a very brief reign, following the Calais-Eurotunnel team time trial. The Belgian would thus pedal in gold, through the English countryside of Kent and East Sussex. He then handed over his place to his teammate Flavio Vanzella for 2 days, so depriving the British riders of glory in their brief sojourn on English soil. Ironically, once back in France, Englishman Sean Yates would take the yellow jersey in Rennes.

In 1996, Frédéric Moncassin had his day of glory. The victory of a French road-sprinter had become a rare

The Dutchman Jan Raas, with many achievements to his name, won the yellow jersey in the prologue at the 1978 Tour.

Gerie Knetemann, a time trial specialist, showed the qualities of an all-round cyclist. Like Raas, he was world champion.

Eric Vanderaerden, one of the best sprinters of the 1980s, twice wore the yellow jersey.

Frédéric Moncassin's consistency in the sprints earned him the yellow jersey in 1986.

Johann Museeuw: he used the bonus sprints to take the supreme emblem in 1993 and 1996.

event. The man from Toulouse won his first Tour stage, at the end of a faultless sprint—'s-Hertogenbosch in the Netherlands. His finish effort took him past Cipollini, then Jeroen Blijlevens and Jan Svorada. The next day, he took 6 seconds in a bonus sprint, then 2 more seconds. At the end of the second stage, he was only 1 second behind Zülle, who won the yellow jersey in the prologue. The next day, placed third in the stage, the bonus finally allowed him to wear the precious yellow jersey for just one day!

In 1997, Cipollini took the lead after winning the first 2 stages. Germany's Erik Zabel won the following day's stage, but Cipollini continued to wear the emblem until the finish of the fifth stage where the reign of Cédric Vasseur commenced.

Zabel eventually took a yellow jersey, but not until the following year—1998—at the end of the second stage, after Boardman's withdrawal following a fall. He wouldn't keep it for very long. A certain Bo Hamburger from Denmark was lying in wait. He knew that the third stage, from Roscoff to Lorient, which crossed Brittany from coast to coast, might suit him well. He thus amassed as many seconds as possible in the bonus sprints and, at the finish in Lorient he had enough seconds to put him in yellow. Alas, the next

day, the Dane had to pack the jersey away in his bag, when the Australian Stuart O'Grady took the lead, in Cholet. A teenage fan of his idol and fellow countryman, Phil Anderson, O'Grady realized a childhood dream. The magic of the yellow jersey was as potent as ever.

Erik Zabel, seen here tangling with Jan Svorada, briefly held the yellow jersey in 1998, but only the green jersey had a lasting place in his wardrobe.

League of Nations

Leaders from around the world

1936 Tour. First stage, from Paris to Lille. The Swiss Paul Egli and the Frenchman Maurice Archambaud broke away in the rain at Carvin. Egli took the yellow jersey.

Previous page: The yellow jersey is a universal emblem and every foreign cyclist dreams of taking it home one day.
(Top row) Dutchman Albertus Geldermans very quickly understood the interest of the situation, placing himself under the orders of Jacques Anquetil, as did Irishman Shay Elliott (here seen next to his team leader and Jean Stablinski in 1963).
(Middle row) Belgian Gilbert Desmet, leader in 1956 then, here, in 1963, had to expand his bar in Roulers because of the surge in fans. As for Dane Jôrgen Pedersen in 1986, he took inspiration from the exploits of Kim Andersen three years before.
(Bottom row) As for the Dutch, they always played the troublemakers, Teun Van Vliet for example (1988). Finally, Alex Zülle, the Swiss, the man whose hopes were constantly dashed.

Marcel Kint. His achievements in the one-day classics are shining examples of their kind. In the Tour de France, he wore the yellow jersey only once, in 1937.

I n times past, the yellow jersey belonged to a privileged class, generally consisting of cyclists from France and countries bordering France. However for many years now, other countries in the world have been open to cycling in general and the Tour de France in particular.

The first Austrian to wear the maillot jaune was Max Bulla, the best known and best cyclist from his country, by his results as much as by his formidable career across Europe. Bulla was the sensation of the 1931 Tour, entering at his own expense essentially just for the ride, but succeeding in winning 3 stages. His victory in Dinan also earned him the yellow jersey for a day. He preceded the first yellow jersey by a German, Kurt Stoepel, who won the second stage from Caen to Nantes in 1932.

Switzerland also got down to drawing up a team for the Tour, enabling Paul Egli to take the first stage from Paris to Lille in the rain in 1936, and thus take the yellow jersey for a day. As for Luxembourg, it had always produced road champions who played an important role in the Tour. The most successful of these was Nicolas Frantz, whom we have mentioned before, but Arsène Mersch and Jean Majérus were another two. The tradition continued after the war with two men who found fame, Jean Goldschmidt and "Bim" Diederich.

Goldschmidt took the yellow jersey in 1950, following his victory in the first stage, lost it to Bernard Gauthier, took it back in the time trial and then ceded it in Angers to Gauthier again. Diederich became leader the following year, winning the second stage, from Reims to Ghent.

The first post-war Tour—1948—was interesting for several reasons. Apart from Vietto and Robic, mentioned previously, Pierre Brambilla made his appearance. An Italian from France, he took the yellow jersey in Saint-Brieuc after the time trial. Total collapse came two days later in the Côte de Bonsecours, on the way out of Rouen. Entering the Parc des Princes 13 minutes after his rival Robic, Brambilla could only watch his triumphant rival dressed in yellow. He, poor wretch, went straight to the cyclists' quarters, sad and alone, and took off his now meaningless jersey.

The first, and ephemeral, Dutch yellow jersey was Wim Van Est; the second, Wout Wagtmans had a rather longer reign. In 1954, his victory in the first stage, from Amsterdam to Antwerp, allowed him to show off his trophy to his compatriots. Louison Bobet snatched it from him to cross Brittany as leader, but in Angers, Wagtmans took it back, only letting it go for good in the Pyrenees. But he had grown attached to the maillot jaune and his number one goal was to get it back.

Wagtmans succeeded again in 1955, after the selective stage from Dieppe to Roubaix, which was won by Antonin Rolland, the very same Rolland who would succeed him as leader the next day, in Metz. Wagtmans persisted, and took the yellow jersey the following year, for the last time. Leader in Aix-en-Provence, after the sixteenth stage, the Dutchman passed on the torch to the future winner of the Tour Roger Walkowiak 4 days from the finish, in the stage from Turin to Grenoble.

Still with the Dutchmen, Albertus Geldermans, a real greyhound, with a notable finesse, took the yellow jersey against his will in 1962, at the end of the sixth stage, from Dinard to Brest. His teammate Rudi Altig was already wearing the treasured jersey and there was no reason to go and steal it from him. But a flowing breakaway formed and his team leader Jacques Anquetil ordered Private Geldermans into action, to go and keep an eye on things up front. He did this so well that at the end of the day he had become race leader. Geldermans was starting to weaken after 10 days of racing, though, which explains why he gave up his jersey in the eighth stage.

The brief reign of Tom Simpson now began. In 1962, he became the first Englishman to wear the yellow jersey, though for just one day, at the finish of the twelfth stage, from Pau to Saint-Gaudens. The *Daily Express,* which until then had devoted only a few lines to the Tour, ran an 8-column wide headline: *"Simpson pedals to glory."*

The first Irishman to wear yellow was the gentle Shay Elliott, in 1963, at the finish of the third stage, from Jambes to Roubaix. The Dublin cyclist won the stage in front of his teammate Jean Stablinski. In the last couple of miles, he gave his breakaway companions the slip, including Henry Anglade, who was already imagining himself wearing yellow.

The right stuff. Jean Majérus from Luxembourg, first yellow jersey in the 1935 Tour. Left: Roger Lapébie.

The Dutchman Wout Wagtmanns was very much attached to the yellow jersey. In 1954, his battles with Bobet provided some great moments.

In 1962, Tom Simpson became the first Briton to take the lead in the Tour. He would never be able to repeat this performance.

An awful destiny awaited Simpson on Mont Ventoux in 1967. Here he is climbing the last few hundred meters of the wooded part. Soon he would reach the open climb to the summit, where he collapsed and died.

Albertus Geldermans, a fragile leader in 1962. He took the yellow jersey on the orders of his team leader Jacques Anquetil.

Elliott made his entry to the Tour de France in rather an unusual way. Having come to France to pursue his career, he signed with AC Boulogne-Billancourt and was authorized to take part in his first Tour de France, in 1956, on a French regional team—an unprecedented event—and not a mixed international team as was generally the case.

In the 1963 Tour, the Belgian Gilbert Desmet succeeded Elliott. In Belgium, many people had the same last name, and so this chap was called Gilbert Desmet I. He came from Roulers and had already worn the yellow jersey for a day in 1956, at the Rouen finish. He then had to wait patiently for 7 years before finding yellow glory again, after a fine performance in the Angers time trial, giving him a long reign from the sixth to the sixteenth stage.

The day of the smaller built cyclists returned with the German Karl-Heinz Kunde, who conquered the yellow jersey at Revel in 1966. Nicknamed "the Yellow Dwarf," because of his size—only 5 feet, 2 inches—and his childish face, he would wear yellow for 5 days in all and, at first, strengthen his position in the general classification during the Vals-les-Bains time trial. After him, the Dutchman Jan Janssen ensured the interregnum before the definitive triumph of Lucien Aimar.

In 1967, the Italian Giancarlo Polidori realized *his* lifetime's dream. At the finish of the third stage, from Caen to Amiens, which was won by his compatriot Marino Basso, he found himself awarded the yellow jersey. For this humble servant of cycling, it was an unhoped-for success. A detail: Jacques Anquetil declared war on him, in Italy, on the pretext that his name resembled Raymond Poulidor's. It was thus unthinkable that Polidori should gain a higher classification in the stages than Anquetil, for it would set the whole of France a-chatter. But poor Polidori didn't catch on to the Frenchman's game at all. One day, on the road, Anquetil struck up a conversation with an Italian cyclist. The exchange was particularly pleasant and, later on, Anquetil asked his teammate Anatole Novak for the name of the cyclist. "What, you don't know it?" cried Novak, "But you've been attacking him every day? It's Polidori." From then on, Anquetil and Polidori became the best of friends.

The Belgian Herman Van Springel is best remembered for his victories in the Bordeaux-Paris classic, 7 in all. It's clear that it is preferable to remember triumph rather than defeat, but the Belgian's biggest defeat was not an ordinary one. At the start of the last stage of the 1968 Tour de France, Van Springel wore the yellow jersey, with a lead of 12 seconds over the Spaniard Gregorio San Miguel and 16 seconds over Jan Janssen. There remained only a 40 mile time trial between Melun and Paris. At the finish, the Belgian was beaten by Janssen, and the Dutchman thus won the Tour by 38 seconds. The image of Van Springel, his head in his hands, crying salty tears over his lost jersey, is still vivid today.

We now come to those who were the devoted teammates of Eddy Merckx, such as Joseph Bruyère, a man of excellent character, who wore the yellow jersey for 8 days in the 1978 Tour. He was no stranger to the yellow jersey, though, having won it before in the 1974 Tour, at the end of the first stage in Saint-Pol-de-Léon. He kept it during a very brief trip to England and still held it when they returned, on the stage from Morlaix to Saint-Malo. But the next day, in Caen, Merck relieved his lieutenant. Everything went according to plan; Bruyère had done his job well.

In 1978, Bruyère belonged to the C & A team. Merckx was now his adviser in the directeur sportif's car. Bruyère took the Pyrenees very well and when his adventure came to an end, after having been floored in the Col du Luitel by the sudden heat, the time he had spent wearing yellow was much longer than he had expected.

In 1980, the reign of his compatriot Rudy Pevenage also lasted for 8 days. Having started his time in yellow in front of his mostly incredulous, compatriots, in Liège, he finished in Laplume, a village of 1000 inhabitants in Lot-et-Garonne. Winner of the second stage, from Frankfurt to Metz, in the rain, he took the leader position the next day, with the help of the intermediate bonus sprints. Pevenage didn't want to give it up too soon. From the North through Picardy, Normandy, Brittany, Charente and Gasconny, the locals cheered on this little Flemish albino, born on the Walloon border.

Pevenage had a devilish capacity for controlling things, just like Phil Anderson. In 1981, Anderson became the first Australian to wear the yellow jersey, on the slopes of Pla-d'Adet, in the sixth stage. Anderson's success came to pass when Hinault set a hellish pace behind Lucien Van Impe, who had already broken away. In the wake of the Breton, there was only one rider who could keep up with the pace set: Anderson. Even better, he attacked, and Hinault had to dig into his reserves to contain the firebrand, who held out to the end, finished second, in front of Hinault, and took the yellow jersey in his first Tour de France. No matter that he lost it the next day, Anderson was elected "Sportsman of the Year" in his country. In 1982, he again earned the yellow jersey, wearing it for 8 days.

Herman Van Springel, confident in the yellow jersey. Never would this all-around cyclist receive the praise he deserved. Alongside him: Lucien Aimar (left) and Ferdinand Bracke.

Bernard Hinault often had much to fear from the foreign legion, represented here by Phil Anderson. The Australian left an impression of an extraordinary fighter.

Ludo Peeters, leader of the 1982 Tour, was the archetypal Flemish cyclist, seemingly resistant to any misfortune.

Kim Andersen, first-ever Danish yellow jersey, in 1983.

Lech Piasecki, the first Eastern European cyclist to become leader of the Tour, at the foot of the Berlin Wall. What a symbol (1987).

That year, Ludo Peeters from Belgium was one of the first leaders of the Tour, which started in Basle, with Hinault winning the prologue and Peeters succeeding the next day as leader. Peeters kept it just for the day, but took the leader position 2 years later, again on the first stage, held in the Paris suburbs. Once more it was only brief, since he ceded it the following day to his teammate Jacques Hanegraaf.

That year, 1983, saw the emergence of Kim Andersen. Across the cobblestones of the North, accompanied by Rudy Matthijs, Andersen won the first-ever Danish yellow jersey and boosted the euphoria of the Coop-Mercier team, winners the previous day of the team time trial. Andersen then set to defending his trophy for as long as possible: 5 days exactly, until Pau, where Sean Kelly succeeded him after stacking up bonus points. The Raleigh and Kwantum teams both had many candidates for the yellow jersey at this time. In 1984, for example, apart from Peeters and Hanegraaf, there was also Adri Van der Poel in Béthune, for just one day and, in 1986, for 2 days, Johan Van der Velde, who ceded it to Jörgen Pedersen, who kept his jersey for the next 5 stages.

Something special came in 1987. In Berlin, at the end of the first stage of the Tour, won by the Dutchman Nico Verhoeven, Lech Piasecki became the first Eastern European cyclist to wear the yellow jersey. He was also the first Polish leader of the Tour. Excellent in time trials, Piasecki used his strength to lead a winning breakaway with 7 other riders. A Polish Tour leader at the foot of the Berlin Wall! What a symbol. But he had acquired a taste for the yellow jersey and would wear it again the following year, for 2 days, in the sixth and seventh stages.

In the 1987 Tour, Piasecki would lose his "knitwear" to another ephemeral leader, the sturdy Swiss Erich Maechler. On the third stage, from Karlsruhe to Stuttgart, two riders found themselves together, the Portuguese Acacio Da Silva and Maechler. Having shaken off the rest of the breakaway group, their success depended on their alliance. They rode without restraint, with Da Silva winning the stage and Maechler the yellow jersey. He would keep it until the tenth stage. As for Da Silva, he would become the first Portuguese to win the yellow jersey, a little later on, in 1989, after the first stage, which he won. He lost it in the fifth stage, a time trial from Dinard to Rennes.

Other unexpected jerseys include the first Canadian to wear the yellow jersey. It was not Steve Bauer, who is better known, but Alex Stieda who, in 1986, was just twenty-five years old. From Vancouver, he was the only Canadian on the

Steve Bauer. He remains the best Canadian cyclist in the history of the Tour.

American 7-Eleven team. Stieda took the yellow jersey after the first stage, from Nanterre to Sceaux, which was won by the Belgian Pol Verschure. Alas, it was only temporary.

The other Canadian, Bauer, also became leader of the Tour, for the first time, in the initial stages. In 1988, Bauer won the first stage, from Pontchâteau to Machecoul, and carried the trophy onwards. The following day, the powerful Panasonic team sounded the charge in the team time trial at Ancenis, and took it off him. From then on, the reign of the Dutchmen started: Teun Van Vliet (3 days), Henk Lubberding (1 day) and Jelle Nijdam (2 days) passed the tunic among themselves.

But Bauer desired just one thing, to win back the coveted jersey. This whole Tour was fought to the second. In the eighth stage, from Reims to Nancy, Bauer slipped into a group of 15 and, at the finish, drove a breech through the Panasonic team's wonderful momentum. He took back the yellow jersey, keeping it for 4 days. He would be the last to wear it before the final winner, Pedro Delgado.

In 1992, Bauer appeared once more in yellow for rather a longer reign this time, after a surprise breakaway in the first stage that had a major influence on the rest of the Tour. Accompanied by Ronan Pensec, Claudio Chiappucci and Frans Maassen, Bauer took 10:35 off the peloton. Bauer, yellow jersey at the Futuroscope finish, would lead the Tour until the ninth stage.

Chiappucci also benefited, and hugely, from this first day's breakaway. He succeeded Pensec, in Villard-de-Lans, at the end of the individual time trial. He wore down his resources by attacking in the stage to Luz-Ardiden and couldn't contain Greg LeMond in the individual time trial at the Lac de Vassivière. The Italian had been the only one to wrestle with the American until the very end.

Claudio Chiappucci, acrobatic leader, heralded the return of the climbers' race. His performance in the mountains boosted the enthusiasm of the *tifosi*.

Evgueni Berzin. His inconsistency in the Tour silenced his fans, who were devoted to the Russian since his victorious Tour of Italy.

INDEX